Two Treatises on the Oneness of Existence by the Moroccan Sufi Aḥmad Ibn ʿAjība

(1747–1809)

تقييدان في

وَحدَةِ الْوُجودِ

لسيدي

أَحمدِ بنِ عَجيبةِ

(١١٦١–١٢٢٤)

حققه وقدم له

الأستاذ جان لويس ميشون

وترجمة إلى الإنكليزية

السيد داڤد ستريت

أركيتيپ

Two Treatises on

the Oneness of Existence

by the Moroccan Sufi

Aḥmad Ibn ʿAjība

(1747–1809)

Arabic text edited, translated and presented by

Jean-Louis Michon,

Foreword by Claude Addas

Translated from the French by

David Streight

ARCHETYPE

This first English edition published in 2010 by
ARCHETYPE
Chetwynd House, Bartlow
Cambridge CB21 4PP, UK
www.archetypebooks.com

Originally published in French and Arabic in 1998 as
Taqyīdāni fi waḥdat al-wujūd

ISBN HB: 978 1 901383 39 3
ISBN PB: 978 1 901383 15 7

British Library Cataloguing in Publication Data
A catalogue record for this book is available from
The British Library

This book was designed and set
by Robert Bringhurst at the DecoType headquarters in Amsterdam.
The Arabic type is *Tasmeem Naskh,* created by Thomas Milo & Mirjam Somers.
The Latin type is *Dante,* drawn in Verona by Giovanni Mardersteig,
cut in steel in Paris by Charles Malin, and later digitized
in England by the Monotype Corporation.

Printed and bound in Great Britain

Contents

Foreword

*Ibn ʿAjība is one of the most remarkable spiritual intellectuals Morocco ever produced. A prolific writer, he excelled in both the inward and the outward sciences of Islam and is noted for some of the most outstanding commentaries on classical texts in which he used first a classical exoteric approach and then delved into the hidden meanings. His Sufic commentary on Ibn Ājurrūm's classical text on grammar is a testimony to his genius. He is perhaps most noted for his commentary on the Aphorisms of Ibn ʿAṭaʾ Allāh, known as 'Awakening the Aspirations through Commmentary on Ibn ʿAṭaʾ Allāh's Ruminations'. He was also a master jurist and a scholar of the prophetic literature (*ḥadīth*). His commentary on the Qurʾān is a blend of inward and outward meanings and is noted for his powerful insights into the spiritual power of the text. His section on the *Fātiḥah* *covers the Ninety-nine Names and is one of the most exhaustive studies of the Names ever written. His basic orientation was of the Shadhili school of *taṣawwuf*, which is known for its strict observance of the law as well as its intellectual and academic adherents. Like many later Shadhilis, he was influenced heavily by the thought and writings of Shaykh Muḥyī al-Dīn Ibn al-ʿArabī, the thirteenth-century Andalusian scholar, whose work the *Makkan Openings* *is considered the greatest philosophical exposition of Sufism ever penned. It is, however, a controversial work and was largely set aside in favour of the more orthodox *Iḥyāʾ* *of Imam al-Ghazāli. Perhaps the most complex aspect of the Shaykh's thought is the relationship of creation to the Creator, a central problem in all monotheistic traditions. In these two short treatises the Shaykh Ibn ʿAjība attempts to explain this relationship.*

SHAYKH HAMZA YUSUF · *Zaytuna Institute*

* تمهيد بقلم الأستاذة كلود عداس

حتى إلى أمد قريب، لم تحظ مؤلفات الشيخ ابن عجيبة بعناية الباحثين فى الدراسات الإسلامية بل وكان اسمه لا يعدو أن يوحى بذكر شخصية غير واضحة المعالم لمؤلف صوفى من الطبقة الثانية بالمغرب فى القرن الثامن عشر الميلادى. إن رسالة عبد الخالق جان لويس ميشون الجامعية التى ناقشها سنة ١٩٦٦ وتم نشرها سنة ١٩٧٣،[1] ليس لها الفضل فقط فى رفع النقاب عن شخصية كانت فى ذات الوقت من كبار شيوخ التربية وصاحب التآليف الفريدة ذات الشأن المعتبَر عند أهل التصوف.

نعم، إن هذا العمل عندما كُمِّل بعد سنوات بترجمة فهرسة الشيخ ابن عجيبة،[2] أضاء قسطا مهما من تاريخ التصوف الإسلامى. فأظهر ببداهة، من جهة حيوية التصوف الذى نُعِتَ بالانحطاط زعما فى ذلك الزمن بالمغرب، ومن جهة أخرى برهن على استمرار تأثير ابن العربى على علم التصوف، بعد مرور أزيد من خمسة قرون على وفاته. نلمس هذا من خلال هاتين الرسالتين القصيرتين مثلا. سيكون من قبيل المبالغة لو قدمنا هذين التقييدين كأعمال كبرى للمدرسة الأكبرية، نسبة للمذهب الصوفى الذى أسَّس له ابن العربى الملقب بالشيخ الأكبر. ويبقى أن ابن عجيبة مع إقراره لنسبه الشريف من الناحية الطينية لم يفصح أبدا ولو علانية على الأقل، بنسبه لابن العربى من الناحية الروحية.

وهكذا نبحث بدون جدوى فى مضان الرسالتين عن أقل تلميح لصاحب الفتوحات المكية، تلك الموسوعة الكبرى لديوان المعارف الصوفية لابن العربى التى ظهرت بصفة لا رجعة فيها على الروحانية الإسلامية. ومما يثير الانتباه أكثر، عدم استعمال الشيخ ابن

Preface

Until quite recently, Ibn ʿAjība's work was paid little attention by scholars of Islam. At most, he was considered a relatively unknown minor writer on Sufism in eighteenth-century Morocco. We are thus indebted to Jean-Louis Michon, whose thesis – which he defended in 1966 and published in 1973[1] – introduced to us an individual who was both a spiritual master of considerable breadth and a prolific author whose works are held in high esteem by Muslim spiritual masters.

Michon's work was later augmented by his translation of Ibn ʿAjība's *Autobiography,*[2] which opened not just a new page, but rather a whole new chapter in the history of Islamic mysticism. It brought to light both the vitality of a Sufism that some felt had been in decay during this particular period of Maghreban history, and – in this case through two short metaphysical treatsies by Ibn ʿAjība – Ibn ʿArabī's enduring influence on mystical thought, over five centuries after his death.

It would certainly not be fair to present these short works – which Michon offers in a bilingual edition – as major texts in the 'Akbarian' tradition, meaning the mystical current fathered by Ibn ʿArabī, who is called *al-Shaykh al-Akbar* – the Greatest Master – by his disciples. Moreover, even though it assumes he belonged to the Prophet's genealogy, Ibn ʿAjība never does claim, at least overtly, spiritual descendance from Ibn ʿArabī.

A search for the slightest reference to the *Futūḥāt makkiyya* (Ibn ʿArabī's mystical *summa*, which left a lasting mark on Islamic spirituality) in these two works would be fruitless. But what is even more remarkable is that, with perhaps two exceptions, the technical

عجيبة للاصطلاحات الصوفية الأكبرية وهى التى دخلت على اللغة العربية بكثرة وذلك منذ نهاية القرن الثالث عشر الميلادى. وبالرغم من عدم ظهور الاصطلاحات الأكبرية هنا، فإن المفاهيم التى تؤديها هى حاضرة.

هكذا فالرسالة الأولى تدور حول مفهوم التجلى - وهو من جملة الاصطلاحات الأكبرية، الذى يعد فى مركز الصدارة فى ظهور مراتب الوجود عند الشيخ الأكبر. وكما هو الشأن لدى شيوخ المذهب الأكبرى، ولو بطريقة مبسطة عند ابن عجيبة، فهذا الأخير يفرق بين وجهتين أساسيتين للوجود المطلق: ما يسميه ابن عجيبة «الخمرة الأزلية فى حال الكنزية» من جهة و«الخمرة الأزلية» - الحق - من حيث تجليها بإظهارها للأسماء الإلهية، من جهة أخرى.

تُحيلنا كلمة «الكنزية»، كما هو معلوم، على رمزية ضالعة الحضور فى مؤلفات محيى الدين بن العربى، إشارة إلى الكنز المخفى الذى جاء فى الحديث القدسى، وهو حديث غالبا ما اعتبره العلماء حديثا موضوعا.[٣]

من الناحية الوجودية، يُشير «الكنز المخفى» لتوحيد الكثرة ويطابق عند ابن العربى كما هو الشأن عند ابن عجيبة[٤] مرتبة الألوهية من حيث اشتمالها على كل تعينات الأسماء والصفات الإلهية [فى حال البطون] وعليه وجب تمييزها عن وحدة الذات المطلقة العلية المنزهة عن كل تعدد.[٥]

وينص كلام الشيخ ابن عجيبة على أن ذوات التجليات لا يلحقها حدوث بإظهارها لشمائل «الكنز» حيث يقول «فلما كانت قبل التجلى لا شىء معها، كذلك هى بعد التجلى لا شىء معها إذ تلونها وتشكيلها لا يخرجها عن أصلها من الوحدة فافهم» تَتبيَّن هنا أحد محاور إيجاد مراتب الوجود الذى ورد غير ما مرة عند الشيخ الأكبر، فهو ما فتئ يؤكد أن

vocabulary Ibn ʿAjība uses here is not the vocabulary Ibn ʿArabī bequeathed to the Arabic language in the late thirteenth century. However, even though several terms specific to the Shaykh al-Akbar's terminology are nowhere to be found, the ideas they encompass are very much so.

The first treatise deals with the idea of theophany – *tajallī*. This word is one from Ibn ʿArabī's lexicon. The concept is central to Ibn ʿArabī's idea of cosmogenesis. Like all adherents to Ibn ʿArabī's school, although in his case he does so somewhat summarily, Ibn ʿAjība draws a distinction between two fundamental aspects of Absolute Being: that of *Deus absconditus,* which corresponds to what Ibn ʿAjība calls the 'non-manifested' Essence (*fī ḥāl al-kanziyya*), and that of *Deus revelatus,* which refers to God as He epiphanizes Himself, or manifests His Names. The adjective *kanziyya* refers to a symbol that is ubiquitous in Ibn ʿArabī's works: the 'Hidden Treasure' (*kanz*), the scriptural source for which lies in a *ḥadīth qudsī* (thus, God's own words) that the *ʿulama'* generally consider apocryphal.[3]

Ontologically, the 'Hidden Treasure' refers to the 'Oneness of multiplicity,' which for both Ibn ʿArabī and Ibn ʿAjība[4] corresponds to the Deity in that it includes inner determinations, which the Divine Names or Attributes are; they must thus be distinguished from 'Absolute Oneness', the Oneness of the Essence in its transcendent nakedness: simple in the strictest sense, exclusive of any plurality.[5]

Ibn ʿAjība does stress that the radical simplicity of the Essence is not affected by the unfolding of theophanies as they manifest the riches that the 'Treasure' contains: 'Just as there was nothing with the Essence before theophanic revelation, so is there nothing with it after revelation...' What we see here is a recurrent theme in Ibn ʿArabī's cosmogony, which relentlessly maintains that the multiplicity of theophanies leaves the Oneness of 'Him Who epiphanizes' intact. God is, simultaneously, both immanent and transcendent; as antithetical

تعدد التجليات الإلهية يبقى دون وحدة «الذى يتجلى» لأنه الله تعالى فى ذات الآن قريب ومنزه، وبالرغم من تضاد هاتين الوجهتين الإلهيتين، فهما تجتمعان عند من يجمع الضدين أصالة فـ ﴿هو الأول والآخر والظاهر والباطن﴾ (سورة آل عمران: ٥٧) وعلى هذا المنحى الأكبرى يشرح ابن عجيبة الحديث الشريف « كان الله ولا شىء معه »[٦]. فالمخلوقات التى هى الأوانى هى بالله من حيث هو الأول، ظهرت فيها آثار الأسماء. لكن، كما يأخذ الماء شكل الآنية التى تحتويه دون مساس بجوهره، تتشكل التجليات بمحل ظهورها دون مساس بالتنزيه المطلق للواحد الاحد فالمفهوم المعبَّر عنه عند ابن العربى من خلال «الكنز المخفى» يرتبط بمفهوم «النَّفَس الرحمانى» الذى يقيم الصلة باعتبار ما بين «الخفاء» الإلهى و«الظهور» الإلهى[٧].

إن محبة الله فى الظهور كما ورد فى الحديث القدسى «...فأَحببتُ أن أُعْرَف» أوجدت تنفسا كونيا ظهرت صورته فى العَمَاء التى يصطلح عليها الشيخ ابن عجيبة «بالقبضة»[٨]. فكما تقرر الأمر عند الشيخ ابن العربى بنعته العماء «بالحقيقة المحمدية» وكذلك «بالإنسان الكامل»، نجد الشيخ ابن عجيبة يعادل اصطلاح «القبضة»، «بصورة محمد» عليه الصلاة والسلام أو «بآدم الأكبر»[٩]. لكن ما يلفت النظر بهذا الصدد، تفادى الشيخ ابن عجيبة ذكر الأحاديث التى يستند إليها مفهوم «الحقيقة المحمدية»[١٠]. فبصفته فقيه لا تخفى عنه، طبعا، هذه الأحاديث النبوية، كما لا يخفى عنه إنكار الفقهاء علماء الرسوم «لتفسيرها» المتداول عند مشايخ الصوفية المسلمين[١١]. وعلى كل حال فمؤلف الرسالتين وضعهما بعد ثمان سنوات من سجنه ومحنته بسبب إنكار وتشدد علماء مدينة تطوان...

على الأقل نتساءل أنُسَلِّم قطعا بتأثير ابن العربى على ابن عجيبة ؟

إن المفهوم الذى تدور حوله هاتان الرسالتان، مفهوم وحدة الوجود وما تعلق بها

as these two characteristics might be, they do come together in He who is by essence the coincidence of opposites: 'He is the First and the Last, the Apparent and the Hidden' [Q. 57:3].

Quite characteristic of Ibn ʿArabī's teaching, Ibn ʿAjība interprets the *ḥadīth* 'God is (was) and nothing with him'[6] in this same light. In His being the 'Apparent', God is in solidarity with creatures who are the receptacles (to the term so frequently used by Ibn ʿArabī – *maẓhar*, pl. *maẓāhir* – Ibn ʿAjība prefers *awānī*) that refract His Names. But, just as water necessarily takes the shape of its container without this affecting its intrinsic nature, so also do theophanies mould to the conditioned form of the 'places of manifestation' that receive them, and which they induce without this altering the absolute transcendence of the One God.[7]

In Ibn ʿArabī, the idea of *Deus absconditus* that the symbolism of the 'Hidden Treasure' expresses has a corollary in the *nafas rahmānī*, the breath of the All Merciful, which, in a way, brings about the transition between the 'Hidden' God and the 'Apparent' God. God's irrepressible desire to reveal Himself generates a cosmic sigh in which the 'Cloud' (*al-ʿamāʾ*), that is, prime matter, which Ibn ʿAjība calls the 'Handful' (*al-qabḍa*), takes shape.[8] Just as Ibn ʿArabī equates this 'Cloud' with the 'Muhammadan Reality', or with the 'Perfect Man', Ibn ʿAjība compares the 'Handful' to 'Muhammad's Form', or to the 'Great Adam'.[9] In this case, what is remarkable is that Ibn ʿAjība refrains from reporting the *ḥadīths* upon which the idea of the 'Muhammadan Reality' is based.[10] Given his training as a jurist, he clearly was fully aware of these famous 'sayings' of the Prophet; and he could not have been unaware of the condemnation the Doctors of the Law had levied upon the esoteric interpretation Muslim mystics had given them.[11] He did, after all, compose these lines eight years after a stint in prison that was engendered by the rigid dogmatism of the Tetouan *ʿulamaʾ*.

من مفاهيم أخرى وخصوصا التجليات والحقيقة المحمدية لا يُخَلِّف مجالا للشك فى هذه المسألة. ولو حصل، هل يعنى أن ابن عجيبة كانت له إحاطة بتآليف ابن العربى ؟ نقول، إن الاصطلاحات المستعمَلة تتميّز بوضوح عن تلك التى يستعملها عادة شرح ابن العربى ويزيد فى استبعاد حصول هذه الإحاطة، تلك الكيفية الخافتة المتحرِّزة فى تقديمه لتعاليم ابن العربى بشأن المراتب الوجودية والكونية.

لكن تقرر من جهة أخرى أن ابن عجيبة قد وقف على كتاب «منتهى المدارك» للفرغانى[١٢] الذى افتتح شرحه على تائية ابن الفارض بمدخل منهجى حول المذهب الأكبرى الذى أخذه عن صدر الدين القونوى أكبر تلاميذ ابن العربى، هذا زيادة على معرفته بتآليف الجيلى أحد رؤوس المدرسة الأكبرية حيث ذكره فى التقييد الأول. وأما الجيلى نجده قد خصص أربعة أبواب متتالية من كتابه «الإنسان الكامل» لثلاث مسائل تُهذب الرسالة الثانية، توحيد الأفعال وتوحيد الصفات وأخيرا توحيد الذات. وعليه لا يستبعد أن يكون ابن عجيبة قد تَعَمَّد عدم الإشارة علنا لمذهب «وحدة الوجود» المختلَف فيه. ونُذكِّر أن مثل هذه المداراة عمل بها مؤلفون آخرون قبله وبعده.[١٣]

وتبقى مؤلفات الشيخ ابن عجيبة مثالا لتلك الآثار الأدبية الصوفية العديدة التى ساهمت دونما ضجيج ولكن بنجاعة فى نفس الوقت، فى نشر تعاليم الشيخ الأكبر بكل أنحاء دار الإسلام متفادية على الدوام عدم التصريح بانتصارها لمذهبه.

ترجمة جعفر الكنسوسى

What, at least, is certain is that Ibn ʿAjība was influenced by Ibn ʿArabī. The key idea underlying both these treatises – that of the Oneness of Being and the ideas that support it, especially those relating to theophanies and the 'Muhammadan Reality' – leave no doubt about the matter. But did he have *direct* knowledge of Ibn ʿArabī's work? The terminology he uses – terminology clearly different from that traditionally seen in Ibn ʿArabī's commentators – and the cursory, one might even say watered down, outline he offers of Ibn ʿArabī's teachings on ontology and cosmology, leave this in doubt.

What has been established, on the other hand, is that Ibn ʿAjība had read Farghānī's *Muntahā al-madārik*;[12] Farghānī offers a methodical outline of the Shaykh al-Akbar's teachings that Qūnāwī – Ibn ʿArabī's most noted follower – had passed on to him. As he mentions incidentally in the first treatise, he also knew Jīlī's work, and Jīlī was a key representative of Ibn ʿArabī's school. Jīlī had devoted four chapters in the *Insān kāmil* to the three key ideas of the second treatise: the Oneness of Acts, the Oneness of Attributes, and the Oneness of Essence. Nor can we rule out the possibility that Ibn ʿAjība deliberately blotted out any specific reference to the school of *waḥdat al-wujūd*, given how controversial it was; as we know, the tactic was used by authors both before, and after, his time.[13]

Whatever the case, Ibn ʿAjība's work is eminently representative of this abundant mystical literature which, without ever openly announcing its sympathy for Ibn ʿArabī, did discretely, but effectively, spread the Greatest of Masters' teachings to the four corners of the Islamic world.

CLAUDE ADDAS

ملاحظات

١ انظر فهرس الكتب بالفرنسية صفحة ٢٤.

٢ نفس المصدر.

٣ انظر بخصوص حديث الكنز المخفي عند ابن العربي كتاب الفتحات المكية طبعة بولاق سنة ١٣٢٩ الهجرة، ج II ص ٢٣٢.

٤ انظر الفقرة حيث يقول «وهذه الخمرة أيضا في حال الكنزية كانت متصفة بجميع صفاتها الأزلية، متسمية بأسمائها القدسية» ص رقم ٤٠.

٥ بشأن الفرق عند الشيخ الأكبر بين هاتين المرتبتين الوجوديتين الوحدة المطلقة وتوحيد الكثرة انظر كتاب فصوص الحكم طبعة بيروت سنة ١٩٨٠، ج I ص ١٠٥.

٦ كان فعل ماضي ناقص عند اللغويين، أما عند الشيخ ابن العربي فهو ليس كباقي الأفعال، بل اعتبره، حرفا وجوديا للدلالة على الماضي والحاضر والمستقبل في ذات الوقت فهو يستشرف الزمن البشري ليشير للحضور الديمومي الإلهي.

٧ انظر كتاب الفتوحات المكية ج II ص ٥٩٧.

٨ انظر كتاب الفتوحات المكية ج II ص ١٢٣، ٣١٠، ٤٥٩؛ ج III ص ٤٤٣، بشأن مفهوم «العماء» و «نفَس الرحمن» عند ابن العربي.

٩ بشأن مفهوم الحقيقة المحمدية انظر الباب الرابع من كتاب *Le Sceau des Saints,* Michel Chodkiewicz (طبعة باريس ١٩٨٦).

١٠ هنا اكتفى الشيخ ابن عجيبة بقوله « كما في بعض الأحاديث» النبوية ص ٤٨.

١١ انظر كتاب *Le Sceau des Saints* ص ٨٢-٨٠ بشأن هذه الأحاديث والجدل القائم حولها.

١٢ انظر كتاب *Autobiographie du Soufi marocain Ahmed Ibn ʿAjība* ص ١٣٣.

١٣ انظر فيما يخص هذا الموضوع كتاب *Un Océan sans rivage* للأستاذ شودكفيتش (طبعة باريس ١٩٩٢) ص ٣٢-١٨.

NOTES

1 See Bibliography.

2 Idem.

3 On Ibn ʿArabī's concept of the 'Hidden Treasure', cf. *Futūḥāt makkiyya*, ed. Būlāq, 1329 AH, II, pp. 232, 310, 399.

4 Cf. the passage where he states: 'In the unmanifested state, this Wine contains all its eternal attributes, all its Holy Names.' p. 41.

5 On the distinction Ibn ʿArabī makes between these two ontological degrees of Being – 'Absolute Oneness' and 'Oneness of multiplicity' – cf. *Fuṣūṣ al-ḥikam*, Beirut, 1980, I, p. 105.

6 *Kāna*, which is usually translated as 'was', is not a verb properly speaking, as Ibn ʿArabī points out. It is rather an existential particle (*ḥarf wujūd*) that refers to the past and the present as much as it does to the future. Beyond the limits of human time, it refers to the eternal divine Present. Cf. *Futūḥāt* II, 56.692; on this point, see also Baylānī, *Epître sur Unicité Absolue*, trans. M. Chodkiewicz, Paris, 1982, p. 46, note 2.

7 On this subject, cf. *Futūḥāt*, II, p. 597.

8 For more on the concept of 'Cloud' and the 'Breath of the All Merciful' in Ibn ʿArabī, cf. *Futūḥāt* II, pp. 123, 310, 459, 311; III, p. 443.

9 On the idea of the 'Muhammadan Reality,' see M. Chodkiewicz, *Seal of the Saints*, Cambridge, 1993, ch. 4.

10 He limits himself to saying 'as we know from certain *ḥadīths*', p. 49.

11 On these *ḥadīths* and the polemics to which they gave rise, cf. *Seal of the Saints*, pp. 61–63.

12 Cf. *Autobiography of the Moroccan Sufi Aḥmad Ibn ʿAjība*, p. 146.

13 On this subject, see M. Chodkiewicz, *An Ocean Without Shore*, Albany, NY, 1993, pp. 2–14.

Introduction

Fez and the Darqāwa Order

Fertile ground for both scholars and saints, Fez has produced a number of treasures over the course of time. Far from the least of these – in the latter half of the twelfth century in the Islamic calendar (the eighteenth in the Gregorian) – was the *ṭarīqa darqāwiyya*: the esoteric, or Sufi, Darqāwa order, through whose branches and offshoots the sap of rich spiritual life has henceforth flowed throughout the Muslim world.

The brotherhood's founder, Mawlāy al-ʿArabī al-Darqāwī, who died at age 86 in 1239/1823, is well known to students of Muslim esotericism. For this we are especially indebted to Titus Burckhardt's translations of the Letters (*Rasāʾil*) the Sufi master wrote to some of God's 'poor ones' (*fuqarāʾ*), his followers on the path (*ṭarīqa*) of inner purification leading to God.

Mawlāy Darqāwī's teacher, the Idrissid *sharīf* Ali al-Jamal al-ʿAmrānī, was himself a teacher in Fez, where he died in 1194/1780; the zawiya he founded, and in which his tomb is located, has been a meeting point for the Darqāwa 'brothers' (*ikhwān*) since that time, and is used regularly for their meditation (*dhikr*) and ecstatic dance (*raqs*, *ʿimāra*).

The initiatory chain (*silsila*) which, from the Prophet Muhammad, through his Companions (*ṣaḥāba*) and their followers (*tābiʿūn*), and then through the masters of the eastern schools in Basra and Kufa, in Khorassan and Baghdad, ultimately brought Mawlāy Darqāwī both the rules and practices of Sufism (*al-taṣawwuf*), and the spiritual influence necessary to allow them to bear fruit in the hearts of those who were on the path (*murīdūn*), already had a number of serious supporters in Morocco. Almost six centuries had passed since ʿAbd al-Salām Ibn Mashīsh (d. 625/1227–28), a descendent of the two Idrises and his disciple Abūl-Hasan al-Shādhilī (d. 656/1258), had established Sufi brotherhoods on the far eastern reaches of the Muslim empire: the Mashīshiyya, or Salāmiyya order, and the Shādhiliyya order, both of which had as much spiritual, as they did intellectual, influence. The Shādhiliyya order recruited a number of its greatest Masters in Fez itself, like Sīdī Yūsuf al-Fāsī (sixteenth century) and his disciple ʿAbd al-Rahmān al-Fāsī al-Fihrī (d. 1100/1680), whose miracles are still spoken of in the city.

Aḥmad Ibn ʿAjība

Mawlāy al-ʿArabī al-Darqāwī had a number of followers, several of whom became 'guides' (*murshidūn*) in their own right, recognized as worthy of leading peers along the path of devotion, of gnosis, and of the love of God: Sīdī Aḥmad b. Muḥammad b. al-Maḥḍī Ibn ʿAjība al-Ḥasanī, the author of the two treatises that appear in the present work, was one of them.

Ibn ʿAjība was born to a *sharīfian* family in Al-Khamīs, in the Jbāla region, in the year 1160 or 1161 (1747–1748). He was educated in Tetouan, and began his own career as a teacher of what were referred to as the 'traditional sciences' at the age of thirty: he taught jurisprudence (*fiqh*), Qurʾānic exegesis (*tafsīr*), dogmatic theology (*usūl al-dīn*), and grammar (*naḥw*) in a number of the city's mosques and madrasas. From 1205 to 1208 (1790–1793) or thereabouts, he made frequent trips back to Fez for the purpose of furthering his studies with famous *ʿulama*ʾ: Muḥammad al-Tawdī Ibn Sūda, Muḥammad Bannīs, Aḥmad al-Zaʿdi, and al-Ṭayyib Ibn Kīrān. He no doubt first heard of Mawlāy Darqāwī during one of these trips and was eager to meet him. Ibn ʿAjība was close to 50 by this time. A number of natural characteristics – his *sharīfian* heritage, his ascetic temperament, his deep piety, and a keen mind focused on the inner essence of things (*al-maʿnā, al-bāṭin*) that lay beneath their outer 'phenomenal' (*al-ḥiss, al-ẓāhir*) surface, in addition to the unflagging ardour with which he had undertaken the practice and study of Islam, even as a child – undoubtedly predisposed him to sense that religion had a deeper dimension, and that this dimension could lead to intimate, permanent contact with God. It was also his hope, as he said, to progress from the domain of speculative knowledge (*ʿilm*) to that of active realisation (*ʿamal*), or from religious law (*sharīʿa*) to the mystical path (*ṭāriqa*), since the latter is what is needed to gain access to Divine Reality (*al-ḥaqīqa*).

Mawlāy al-Darqāwī was no longer residing in Fez when Ibn ʿAjība arrived for his studies. He had left for Bū Brīh (Amjot) years earlier, to found a *zawiya* among the Banī Zarwāl, north-east of Fez, and it was there that he received both followers and visitors who wanted to learn from him. So that is where Ibn ʿAjība went. He told of their meeting in his 'Autobiography' (*Fahrasa,* chapter 8; see below: 'Biographical references'). It was a decisive moment for him, in the sense that, from then on he no longer belonged to himself; although he was initially not fully conscious of the fact, he had just been chosen for a mission quite different from the one he had previously been engaged on; he would go from being a doctor and professor of theology to being a master guide (*shaykh tarbiya*) on the spiritual path.

This transformation could not be completed, however, until Ibn ʿAjība had undergone a rigorous inner and outer ascetic apprenticeship; he had to pass through the narrow gate of *faqr,* spiritual 'poverty', so that he would be able to understand fully the injunction contained in the holy saying: 'God is rich, you are the poor' [Q. 47:38]. The guide who assisted him in crossing the threshold into this purifying stage was not Mawlāy Darqāwī himself, but rather one of his closest disciples, Muḥammad al-Buzīdī al-Ḥasanī, a humble, almost illiterate *sharīf* who lived not far from Tetouan in the land of the Ghmāra. The circumstances of the education Shaykh Buzīdī imparted to his disciple – which saw the latter giving up his teaching positions and his renown as a teacher in order to don the tattered frock (*muraqqaʿa*) of the dervish, and sever his relations with high society in Tetouan – are related in detail in chapter 11 of Ibn ʿAjība's *Fahrasa*. Ibn ʿAjība reached illumination (*fatḥ*) and spiritual mastery in the space of only a year or two; from then until the time of his death (7 *Shawwāl* 1224/15 November 1809) he was to offer edifying proof of his inner development, through both his intense activity as an educator – he spread the *ṭarīqa darqāwiyya* throughout the region of the Jbāla, from Tangiers to Tetouan – and his remarkable literary output.

Even before entering the *ṭarīqa*, Ibn ʿAjība had composed some fifteen works on religious subjects: a treatise on Qurʾānic readings, another on actions and intentions, a collection of biographies of the experts in Malekite law, and even a number of commentaries on devotional and esoteric works, among which were Busīrī's *Hamziyya* and his *Burda*, Aḥmad Zarrūq's *Wazīfa*, Ibn Naḥwī's *Munfarija*, and Imām Shādhilī's *Ḥizb al-Kabīr* (*Ḥizb al-Barr*). None of the works he composed during this period appears to have gained fame, however, and even though some of them have been preserved in manuscript form, none has been honoured by the printed word.[1]

The first works of his 'initiatory' period were commentaries, one on Ibn al-Bannāʾ al-Tujībī's *Mabāḥith al-asliyya*, and the other on Ibn ʿAṭāʾ Allāh of Alexandria's *Ḥikam*. These were followed by a sizeable commentary on the Qurʾān in four volumes (*Al-Baḥr al-madīd fī tafsīr al-Qur'ān al-majīd*), of which only two were first printed in Cairo (in 1375/1955 and 1376/1956) before a full, annotated edition in six volumes was published in Cairo between 1999 and 2001 by Dr Hasan Abbas Zaky. In Ibn ʿAjība's own words, this commentary combines the 'literal method' (*ʿibāra*) of the exotericists with the allusive method (*ishāra*) of the esotericists (*Fahrasa,* chapter 6), which explains why its author has won the esteem and consideration of both Sufis and the doctors of the law. In addition to these three works, which are his most voluminous, Ibn ʿAjība composed some twenty treatises and commentaries on Sufi teachings and the Sufi path, including the two short works that are presented here.

The Two Treatises on the Unity of Existence

These two treatises, or précis (*taqyīd*), were composed in 1216/1801 (according to the date on one of the manuscripts), eight years after Ibn ʿAjība entered the *ṭarīqa,* and eight years before his death. They are thus representative of his fully mature thinking and, as Ibn ʿAjība informs us in his introductory remarks, they are the fruit of his personal spiritual experience.

There is nothing novel about their subject matter: it is the doctrine of the 'Unity of Existence', or 'Unity of Being' (*waḥdāt al-wujūd*) which 'the Greatest of Masters' (*al-shaykh al-akbar*), Muḥyī al-Dīn Ibn ʿArabī, had so brilliantly put into words some five centuries earlier in his 'Meccan Illuminations' (*al-Futūḥāt al-makkiyya*), his 'Bezels of Wisdom' (*Fuṣūṣ al-ḥikam*), and a multitude of other works. Since the time of Ibn ʿArabī, the doctrine has given rise to and nourished so many contemplative vocations, and inspired so many interpreters, that it is no longer possible to separate the work from the study of Sufism (Islam's esoteric dimension) as a whole.

The extent to which Ibn ʿAjība received oral instruction on the Shaykh al-Akbar's works and doctrine, or was even directly aware of his writings, is uncertain. Although the questions have been raised, I have never been able to respond with anything other than a plea of ignorance. Ibn ʿAjība mentions Ibn ʿArabī in none of the three *Fahrasa* chapters where he lists the teachers from whom he had received teachings and the works – including those on *taṣawwuf*, like Ibn ʿAṭāʾ Allāh al-Iskandarī's *Ḥikam* – that he studied with them. The list of works he authored, which is included in the following chapter (the sixth in the *Fahrasa*), makes but a single reference to a work by Ibn ʿArabī: a *tasliya,* upon which Ibn ʿAjība wrote a nine-page commentary in a manuscript. He also composed a short commentary (five pages) on poetry that some attribute to Ibn ʿArabī, but which he himself claims was written by Junayd. Although my perusal of Ibn ʿAjība's works is far from complete (they total some six thousand pages), I have yet to encounter a direct reference to the Shaykh al-Akbar other than the just mentioned *tasliya,* and it, according to what Ibn ʿAjība says in the beginning of his Commentary, is only 'attributed' to Ibn ʿArabī.[2] In all likelihood, Ibn ʿAjība, who is among those authors who have no hesitation about citing sources for their quotes or paraphrases, was not a frequent peruser of Ibn ʿArabī's works. The two treatises presented here are thus only one example among many of the tremendous influence, over both time and space, that the teachings of 'the Greatest Master' exerted, and continue to exert.

Even if the teaching of the Unity of Existence – or of the 'Oneness of Being', according to the translation adopted by Michel Chodkiewicz in his presentation of a Yemenite treatise that was also inspired by Ibn ʿArabī (see 'Bibliographic References', below, 3) – is a recurrent theme in Sufi literature, there are an infinite number of ways to approach it. The merit of Ibn ʿAjība's two treatises and why they are interesting is due to two things. The first is their conciseness, since it is far from easy to summarize so vast and complex a doctrine in twenty or so handwritten pages. The second is the procedure he followed, a procedure alluded to in the titles of the works, and in the subdivisions of each. Each précis, to a certain extent, forms one panel of a diptych, the first of which contains two pictures, and the second, three; their themes are arranged as follows:

TREATISE I: On the Divine Essence

1) Before it is revealed, that is, in its unmanifested state, of absolute occultation;
2) After the theophanic radiation, which leaves it unchanged and eternally identical to itself.

TREATISE II: Protective Veils that Conceal (and, and at the same time, reveal) the Lord's Nature from the Creature-Servant; this Nature is Unity

1) Unity of Action, for all actions come from God;
2) Unity of Attributes, for all qualities belong to God;
3) Unity of Essence, for God alone is real.

Movement from one treatise to the other is thus bi-directional: the first treatise starts from the point of eternal, absolute Essence (*al-dhāt al-azaliyya, dhāt al-ḥaqq*) and describes how this essence takes formal and restrictive conditions upon itself; it is a metaphysical commentary on the non-duality (*aḥadiyya*) of the Divine Principle in itself, as well as an explanation of the theophanic process (*tajallī*), meaning the self-revelatory process of the ineffable Mystery which, though it is unknowable in itself, can indeed be grasped through its manifestation of itself. The second treatise has its point of departure in the human condition, which is 'created' in the image of God – since creation is nothing other than one mode of theophanic revelation –

and returns to the very source of the birth of existence, the 'Lord', through the removal of the veils of existence; it is a commentary on the doctrine of unification (*ittiḥād*) and the process of return of the form of the creature to the essential Principle.

Thus, the key idea is that of the Divine Essence projecting itself outwardly, since without this projection nothing would exist other than the unqualified, and therefore unknowable, Absolute. Both this idea and the noun denoting it, *tajallī,* come from the Qur'ānic verb *tajallā*, meaning 'to appear' or 'to manifest oneself', seen in the Qur'ān (7:143) when God 'appeared' on Mount Sinai; whence also the Divine Name *al-Mutajallī*, 'The Revealer'. *Tajallī* is thus the process through which the ineffable Mystery radiates outwardly the latent possibilities it has contained for all eternity. The closest translation is through the word 'theophany', which suggests that 'God appears', or, even more explicitly, by an expression like 'theophanic' radiation, since the latter expression entails a manifestation for which God Himself is simultaneously the subject and the object.

Ibn ʿAjība, as had been the case for Ibn ʿArabī (cf. Corbin, *Creative Imagination…*, pp. 190–193), points out that this radiation or theophanic revelation is the result of a tension of desire that arises within the Absolute itself, as seen in the inspired saying (*ḥadīth qudsī*) where God, speaking through Muhammad, declares, 'I was a hidden treasure (*kanz makhfī*). But I longed to be known, so I created the creatures…' This internal tension is concretized in a 'contraction' called 'the Handful' (*al-qabḍa*). This is the first level at which the Essence is determined. It entails both an inner modality – an uncreated divine aspect, an aspect of pure intelligibility (*maʿnā*) – and an outer modality, a creaturely, sensitive aspect (*ḥiss*). What is at issue here is thus the very root of the universe, the unique protoype from which all beings originate, which Ibn ʿAjība also calls 'the Muhammadan form' or 'the great Adam', but which other Sufis, like ʿAbd al-Karīm al Jīlī, have called 'the Perfect Man' (*al-insān al-kāmil*), or, in reference to Greek and Neoplatonic terminology, the 'macrocosm' (*al-ʿālam al-kabīr*).

From this primordial Handful [of Light] gush forth, by effusion, or overflowing (*fayḍ*), the Secrets and Lights, that is to say, the manifestations of the Divine Names and Qualities that are nothing more than refractions of the one original Light. This overflowing spills out over all the planes of existence, thus allowing all the potentialities contained within the Essence to become apparent in distinctive ways. The appearance unfolds neither chronologically nor sequentially, rather it follows a 'logic', in keeping with the very nature of its potentialities: within the *qabḍa,* as within the pure Divine Being, potentialities already possess their specific abilities to receive the inflowing of existence, and they can only be made manifest at the level – and in the order – specific to them.

In the final analysis, the different levels of existence are thus merely the different modalities of self-revelation of the One Essence. In the measure that the Essence only reveals itself to itself, in an exclusively spiritual or intelligible fashion, the mirror in which it sees itself is called the 'world of Divine ideas', or the 'world of spirits', or 'Omnipotence' (*jabarūt*). In the measure that the Absolute assumes a mode of intermediate manifestation – animic or psychic – minds or souls – the level on which it is revealed is called the 'world of souls', the world of 'Royalty' (*malakūt*); it is also, in Ibn ʿArabī's terminology, the domain of the Creative Imagination (*khayal*), the world of symbols (*ʿālam al-mithāl*). Finally, the degree of gross manifestation in which the Absolute takes on the veil of bodily form, is called 'the world of the senses', 'the world of bodies', 'the phenomenal world', 'the Kingdom' (*mulk*), etc. All these expressions are seen in the texts that follow.

Each level of reality, and each reality or particular form situated at this level, is thus a mirror in which the Original Light, which in itself is both invisible and imperceptible, is made manifest ('is known').

A level, or a being – the human being, for example – is said to be a 'place of theophany', a 'revealing form' (*maẓhar*), in the sense that what is considered is its essential aspect, that is, as a reflection of the Absolute. It might also be said that it is a receptacle (*āniya*; pl. *awānī*) in which the undifferentiated Original Light takes on colour, like wine does in a glass; or that it is a veil (*ḥijab*; pl. *ḥujub*), since the brightness of this same Light is mercifully softened in it, so that its 'contours' (*rasm*; pl. *rusūm*) can be brought into existence and remain until such time as it is finally reabsorbed. On the other hand, if we look at the creaturely form from the point of view of its opacity and its individuation, we might see it as a 'mould' (*qālab*; pl. *qawālib*), an image that underscores both the materiality of the 'receptacle' and the specific nature of its 'contour'.

Man, who was created as a summary of the universe and placed at the confluence of all the worlds, has access to all the orders of reality; depending on whether he 'looks' with his external senses (*ẓawāhir*) or whether he uses his internal faculties (*bawāṭin*), he perceives either sensible forms or intelligible realities (*al-maʿānī*; pl. of *maʿnā*). These two modes of knowing are practised on different levels, but they are not necessarily incompatible. They are incompatible only in the sense that a mode of perception becomes exclusive and hides the level of reality that is either above it (in which case man is the victim of his senses, unable to grasp anything other than the outer 'husk' of things) or below it (in which case man, completely absorbed by contemplation of the celestial realities, risks forgetting his terrestrial duties and the statutes of his condition as 'servant'). Thus, the accomplished Sufi is that individual for whom the distinctive perception (*farq*) of beings and things does not constitute a veil that hides the essential unity (*jamʿ*) of these same beings, and vice-versa. He no longer perceives through his own faculties, but rather through an intuitive knowledge (*kashf*) that participates in the revelation that

God desires, as much for His creature as for Himself. For him, there is no longer any opposition between the outer and the inner, between the sensible and the intelligible; there is but a single synthetic vision (*ʿayn al-jamʿ*) of Reality, always identical to itself, in the diversity of its hypostases.

This is the end of the mystical path (*wusūl al-ṭariq*), which retraces, inversely, the process of theophanic revelation. Just as God manifests himself on three levels of existence, the return to Him also entails three stages, which correspond to three different manners of conceiving the essential unity underlying all things (*waḥdat al-wujūd*). Ibn ʿAjība describes them as successive stages of unveiling (revelation) during the course of which man realizes (1) that he is not the master of his acts, or at least that he is in control of them only in an outer, quite limited, and provisional sense; since God is the sole Agent, true freedom consists in watching Him act with His human instrument, and in removing from the human being any pretension of either power or will; (2) that he is not the possessor of what he believes to be 'his' attributes, which are nothing more than the distant, shattered reflection of divine perfections; and (3) that in sum, he possesses no existence and no reality other than that which belongs to the sole true Essence, in which all alterities are effaced and all beautiful qualities become perennial.

Note on the Translation

Such, then, broadly speaking, is the material contained in these two treatises. I felt as though this preliminary outline would afford the best introduction to the treatises since, given his penchant for conciseness, Ibn ʿAjība occasionally presumed both that his readers had a relatively high level of knowledge, and that they would grasp the doctrinal allusions hidden behind the technical references in his work. Since he was addressing followers in esoteric orders, he undoubtedly was of the opinion that they were familiar with Sufi concepts. I must admit that extensive interaction with his writings was necessary before I was fully able to follow the occasionally quite 'abbreviated' train of some of his thoughts, and to reach the point where I could fine-tune the details of my translation.

This translation aims to replicate as closely as possible the author's intention, which was to provide a concise introductory overview of a vast area of subject matter. Caught between wanting to offer a very literal translation on the one hand, in which the extreme conciseness of the Arabic and its use of metaphorical expressions would have been abstruse for western readers, and, on the other, a liberal paraphrase that avoided Sufi vocabulary in favour of terms closer to our philosophical customs, I chose a middle road by opting to respect sentence structure and the author's train of thought, and translating literally the concrete evocative words; but a few annotations were added where needed (these are always indicated by parentheses), and in a few cases equivalent terms (also in parentheses) have been proposed in order to translate technical words in Arabic. This procedure has, therfore, both included explanations to the text and avoided an excess of footnotes. Despite these precautions, the resulting translation runs the risk of being neither appealing, nor easy reading; some may be of the opinion – and rightly so – that more extensive commentary is needed in several places. If such is the case, I urge them to refer to the works listed in the 'Bibliographical References', and for ideas related to technical expressions, in particular, to the glossary at the end of Titus Burckhardt's three works, to the index of technical terms composed by Izutsu, or to my translation of the *Miʿrāj,* a glossary of technical terms in *taṣawwuf* composed by Ibn ʿAjība himself.

The Manuscripts

The translation of the Arabic text of these two treatises is based on two manuscripts:

a) The first is preserved in the Bibliothèque Générale in Rabat, under the code D 1974/4 and 5 (pp. 226–241). It is easily readable, and appears to have been written by an educated Moroccan; it contains very few errors, other than a few omissions and occasional vocalization errors in its poetic citations.
b) The second is from a quite large anthology that is part of an 'endowment body of literature' (*ḥabūs*) belonging to the Hāshimiyya branch of the Darqāwa order in Damascus. There are several other works by Ibn ʿAjība in the same anthology, which were photocopied for me in September, 1964. It was copied by a follower of Shaykh al-Ḥājj Muḥammad al-Habrī, who mentions having completed his task a few days before the death of his master, during Ramaḍān 1317 (January 1900). The Maghrebin spelling is regular, but contracted and there are many morphological errors.

As these two manuscripts offer strictly identical versions of both treatises, I felt justified in deciding against careful comparisons with three other manuscripts also preserved in Morocco:

c) treatise I, in the Bibliothèque Générale in Rabat; in *majmūʿ* K 1146, p. 106–111; this is the manuscript that closes with the words: 'completed Saturday, 16 Jumada II 1216' (24 October 1801); it was copied in 1263/1847.
d) treatise II, in the Bibliothèque Générale in Rabat; in *majmūʿ* D. 2589/2; 8 pages.
e) treatise III, in the Bibliothèque Générale in Tetouan.

NOTES

1 Cf. *Encyclopedia of Islam*, New Edition, article 'Ibn ʿAdjība'.

2 A brochure containing the commentary on this *tasliya* was published in 1402/1982 (the place of publication is not specified, but was probably Morocco) by one of the author's descendants, Aḥmad Muḥammad Ibn ʿAjība.

BIBLIOGRAPHICAL REFERENCES

I. On the Darqāwa

Articles titled 'Darkāwa' in *Encyclopedia of Islam* (EI), 1st and 2nd editions (A. Cour and R. Le Tourneau).

Burckhardt, T. *Letters of a Sufi Master* (partial trans. of Moulay al-ʿArabī al-Darqāwī's *Rasāʾil*). Bedfont, Middlesex, 1973.

Drague, G. *Esquisse d'Histoire religieuse du Maroc.* Paris, 1951 (passim).

Lings, M. *A Sufi Saint of the Twentieth Century: Shaykh Aḥmad al-ʿAlawī.* London, 1971.

Rinn, L. *Marabouts et Khouans.* Algiers, 1884, pp. 231–264.

Trimingham, J.S. *The Sufi Orders of Islam.* Oxford, 1951 (passim).

II. On Ibn ʿAjība

Article titled 'Ibn ʿAdjība', EI2 (J.-L. Michon).

Michon, J.-L. 'L'autobiographie (*Fahrasa*) du Soufi marocain Aḥmad Ibn ʿAjība', in *Arabica* 1969, and E.J. Brill, 1969; 2nd edition, Arché, Milan, 1982; English translation by David Streight, *The Autobiography (Fahrasa) of a Moroccan Soufi: Aḥmad Ibn ʿAjība (1747–1809)*, Louisville, KY, 1999.

Michon, J.-L. *Le Soufi marocain Aḥmad Ibn ʿAjība (1746–1809) et son Miʿrāj, glossaire de la mystique musulmane*, 'Etudes Musulmanes', XIV, Vrin, Paris, 1973, 2nd edition 1990.

III. On Sufi doctrine and the Unity of Being

It would be impossible to list here, even briefly, the numerous works by scholars of Middle Eastern studies on this doctrine in general and its main interpreters, the most notable of whom is Ibn ʿArabī. The following works are suggested because they offer a particularly insightful analysis of some of the doctrine's most important aspects. The works by Corbin, Izutsu and Nasr also contain useful bibliographical information.

Addas, C. *Quest for the Red Sulphur: The Life of Ibn ʿArabi.* Cambridge, 1993.

ʿAfifi, A. *The Mystical Philosophy of Ibnu'l-ʿArabī.* 2nd ed., London, 1964.

Burckhardt, T. *Universal Man.* Partial trans. of ʿAbd al-Karīm al-Jīlī's *al-Insān al-Kāmil,* Sherbourne, 1975.

Burckhardt, T. *An Introduction to Sufi Doctrine.* Trans. D.M. Matheson, Wellingborough, Northamptonshire, 1976.

Burckhardt, T. *Wisdom of the Prophets* (partial trans. of Ibn ʿArabī's *Fuṣūṣ al-ḥikam,* English trans. by Angela Culme-Seymour. Beshara Publications, 1975).

Chodkiewicz, M. Emir ʿAbd al-Kader, *Ecrits spirituels.* Paris, 1982 (especially ch. 2, 'De l'unicité de l'être').

Chodkiewicz, M. *Un traité yéménite sur l'unicité de l'être,* in the magazine *Horizons maghrébins,* no. 30, 1995.

Corbin, H. *Creative Imagination in the Sufism of Ibn ʿArabī.* English trans. by Ralph Manheim, Princeton, 1969.

Izutsu, T. *Unicité de l'existence et création perpétuelle en mystique islamique,* trans. from English by Charlotte Grandy, 'Les deux océans'. Paris, 1980.

Nasr, Seyyed Hossein. *Three Muslim Sages,* Cambridge, MA, 1964 (see pp. 104–116, an outline of the *Unity of Being* according to Ibn 'Arabī, where the author refutes the use of the term 'pantheism' that some Orientalist authors have applied to the doctrine).

Schaya, L. *La doctrine soufique de l'Unité.* Paris, 1962 (chapter 4 of which outlines the doctrine of the creation as *tajallī,* in accord with Ibn ʿArabī's teachings).

Schuon, F. *L'Oeil du Coeur.* Paris, 1974 (see especially the chapter titled 'En-Nūr', where teachings on divine self-determination and the different levels of manifestation are outlined).

Schuon, F. *Understanding Islam*. Bloomington, IN, 1998. (An overview in which the author, without attempting a systematic outline, applies the metaphysical criteria of *waḥdat al-wujūd* to aspects of Islam and Muslim spirituality; the passages on the Prophet as totality and 'origin' are a valuable complement to what Ibn ʿAjība's second treatise says regarding the *qabḍa muḥammadiyya*).

NOTE ON THE EDITOR/TRANSLATOR FROM ARABIC

Jean-Louis Michon, born in Nancy (France), studied liberal arts, law, and political science, earning a doctoral degree in Islamic Studies in Paris. He also studied architecture and was a practising architect in Switzerland before beginning tenures with a number of organizations connected to the United Nations. As UNESCO expert for the Moroccan government, a post he held from 1972 until 1979, he took part in establishing programs cataloguing and preserving Morocco's cultural heritage: historical monuments, sites, and traditional arts and crafts.

❁ I ❁

التقييد الأول

* في حال الذات الأزلية قبل التجلي وبعده

الحمد لله الواجب الوجود المتجلي بكل موجود والصلاة والسلام على بذرة الوجود ومنبع المكارم والجود سيدنا محمد أفضل كل حامد ومحمود.

وبعد فهذه نبذة من نعوت الخمرة الأزلية قبل التجلي وبعده، حملني على جمعها ما وقع فيها من الخوض من بعض الإخوان من غير دليل منهم ولا برهان، فأردت أن أبين ما أدركته الأكوان السليمة، والنقول المستقيمة، يكون ذلك بإشارة لطيفة، وألغاز رقيقة، لأن علمنا كله إشارة فإذا صار عبارة خفي. وبالله أستعين ولا حول ولا قوة إلا بالله العلي العظيم.

* نعوت الخمرة في حال الكنزية

كانت الخمرة الأزلية قبل أن تجلى في الأواني، لطيفة المباني، نورانية شعشعانية، روحانية بلاجسمانية، أولية بلا بداية، آخرية بلانهاية، ليس لها حصر ولا غاية، لا يمكن لأجل لطافتها

On the Eternal Essence before and after Theophanic Revelation

Praise be to God, the Necessary Being who reveals Himself through every existing thing! Prayer and salutation to the seed of existence, the source of virtue and generosity, our lord and teacher Muhammad, the most noble of all who praise, and the most worthy of being praised!

If I have been led to compose this brief outline of the characteristics of the Eternal Wine[1] before and after theophanic revelation, it is because of discussions on the subject that have arisen among followers incapable of demonstrating and offering evidence for their claims. I thus decided to explain what true intuitions[2] have grasped and what trustworthy traditions have confirmed. This explanation is offered with subtle references and enigmatic touches, because our knowledge is entirely allusive, and because, to the extent that it becomes expressive, it hides itself. May God be my succour; there is no power or strength but in Him, the Most High, the Magnificent!

On the Characteristics of the Essence in the State of Non-manifestation[3]

Before it reveals itself in receptacles, the Eternal Essence is[4] of a subtle, luminous, radiant, spiritual structure without corporality; it is first, without a beginning; it is last, without an end; it has neither limit nor term; its subtlety[5] prevents eyes from perceiving it and sciences and thought from embracing it. In the state of non-manifestation, it allows no form (*shakl*), no limitation (*rasm*), no substance (*jawhar*), no body (*jism*); it is nothing but pure intelligibility (*maʿānī ṣāfiya*), with no aspect (*ḥiss*) that can be grasped by the senses; it is total Lordship (*rubūbiyya*), with no element of servitude (*ʿubūdiyya*), since the state

أن تدركها الأبصار، ولا تحيط بها العلوم والأفكار، وليس لها فى حال الكنزية شكل ولا رسم ولا جوهر ولا جسم. وإنما هى هناك معانى صافية لا حس فيها، وربوبية محضة لا عبودية فيها، لأن العبودية من وظائف الأشكال والرسوم، وليس هناك إلا أسرار الحى القيوم، وإنما ظهرت الأشكال والرسوم فى الخمرة بعد تجليها ووضعها فى الكيسان، ليشربها منها أهل العرفان، فلما ظهرت الخمرة فى الأشكال والرسوم، كساها رداء الكبرياء والعز الحى القيوم، وهى أوصاف البشرية، وأحكام العبودية، فهى فى حال الكنزية غنية عن الرداء، فالعروسة قبل أن تجلى لا تحتاج إلى رداء. نعم العلم بظهور العبودية قديم، وكذلك المعانى التى هى مادة الأشكال والرسوم، وظهور نعوت العبودية حادثة، وهى تلوين للخمرة واحتجاب لها بعد ظهورها، ليبقى السر مصونا، والكنز بعد الظهور مدفونا، وليتحقق فيها اسمه الظاهر والباطن. فلا حدوث عندنا فى ذوات التجليات التى هى مظاهر الخمرة، وإنما الحدوث فى تلونها وتشكيلها بعد ظهورها، وليس ذلك التلوين والتشكيل شيئا زائدا عليها. فلما كانت قبل التجلى لا شىء معها، كذلك هى بعد التجلى لا شىء معها، إذ تلونها وتشكيلها لا يخرجها عن أصلها من الوحدة

of servitude is a condition inherent in formal, limited things. Here (in the non-manifested Essence), there is nothing but the secrets of the Living One, the Self-Subsisting One.

If formal, limited things have become visible after the Eternal Wine – in the process of revealing itself – has filled and coloured the cups (*al-kisān,* meaning the forms of the manifested universe), it is only so that gnostics might be able to drink of the Wine. When the Eternal Essence thus appears in formal, limited things, it is clothed in the mantle of lordly grandeur and glory, which is immediately identified with the attributes of human nature and with the laws that govern the state of servitude. However, in the unmanifested state, the Eternal Essence has no more need of a cloak than a bride does on her wedding night.

Indeed, manifestation of the state of servitude has been known (in God's Omniscience) from all eternity, just as intelligible realities (the 'Divine Ideas': *al-maʿānī*), which are the archetypes (*mādda*) of formal determinations, are eternal; manifestation of the characteristics of the state of servitude is contingent, however. These characteristics are the very colouring (*talwīn*)[6] of the Eternal Wine, a veil that hides it after it has been opened to the light of day, so that it remains a well-guarded secret and a buried treasure, and also so that the truth of the Divine Names 'the Apparent' and 'the Hidden', in them and through them, might be realised. In our opinion, there is no contingency *per se* in the archetypes that are the places where the Essence is manifested; rather, there is contingency only where the Wine is coloured and takes on a formal (*tashkīl*) determination by manifesting itself, since this colouring and this formal determination are not added to it in any way. Just as there was nothing with the Essence before its theophanic revelation, so is there nothing with it after revelation: no colour, no formal determination can remove it from its primordial Unity (*al-Waḥda*). Let us be certain we understand this!

فافهم. وهذه الخمرة أيضا في حال الكنزية كانت متصفة بجميع صفاتها الأزلية، متسمية بأسمائها القدسية، ثم ظهرت[1] بعد تجليها، آثار أسمائها وصفاتها في مظاهر الأشياء، وشواهد هذه النعوت من طريق النقل قوله صلى الله عليه وسلم «كان الله ولا شيء معه»، أي ليس معه في الأزل شيء ولا رسم ولا العارفين «وهو الآن على ما عليه كان»، أي لأن ما ظهر من الأواني هو من غير المعاني، فما ظهر في عالم الشهادة هو عين الغيب من غير زيادة، وتلوين الخمرة وتحسيسها لا يخرجها عن أصلها كما تقدم. فالأمر الآن على ما كان عليه في الأزل، وفي حديث الترمذي عن أبي رُزَيْن العقيلي، قلنا «يا رسول الله أين كان ربنا قبل أن يخلق خلقه ؟» قال «كان في عماء[2] ليس فوقه هواء ولا تحته هواء»، أي كان في خفاء ولطافة لم يحصره هواء من فوقه ولا من تحته، إذ لا فوق ولا تحت بل هو أوسع من كل فوق ومن كل تحت. قال تعالى ﴿ فأينما تولوا فثَم وجه الله إن الله واسع عليم﴾. وقيل لسيدنا علي كرم الله وجهه «يا ابن عم رسول الله أين كان ربنا وهل له مكان ؟» فتغير وسكت ساعة ثم قال «قولكم أين الله ؟ سؤال عن مكان، وكان الله ولا مكان، ثم خلق الزمان والمكان، وهو الآن كما كان، دون زمان

In the unmanifested state, this Wine contains all its eternal attributes, all its Holy Names. After theophanic revelation, the traces (*athār*) of its Names and Attributes appear in the substrates of things (that is, in the forms of creatures, in the sense that it is in them that the Divinity reveals itself). Traditional testimony regarding these characteristics is provided by the words of the Prophet: 'God was, and nothing [was] with Him,' meaning: With Him, in eternity, there is neither form nor delimitation, nor sensory aspect, nor category. One of the gnostics added: 'And He is now even as He was', meaning that what we see in the receptacles comes from the archetypes themselves, that what appears in the phenomenal world (*ʿālam al-shahāda*) is nothing other than (that which is already in) the invisible world (*al-ghayb*), with no increase, and that the fact that the Wine has taken on colour and has become perceptible (*tahsīs*) does not take it out of its original state, as we have already seen: reality is now just as it was for all eternity.

Tirmīdhī reports a *ḥadīth* from Abū Ruzayn al-ʿUqaylī: 'We said to the Prophet, 'Where was our Lord before He created His creation?' He was in a cloud (*ʿamāʾ*) above which there was no atmosphere (*hawāʾ*) and beneath which there was no atmosphere', which means the same as: He was in a dark void (*khafāʾ*), a subtlety limited by no atmosphere above or below it; there is nothing above God, or beneath (Him), as He is vaster than any above or any below. He said: 'Wherever you turn, there is the Face of God; indeed, God is infinitely vast and omniscient' [Q. 2:115].

Someone asked Sayyidnā ʿAlī, 'O cousin of God's Messenger, where is our Lord? Is there some place (*makān*) He is found?' His countenance changed as he fell silent for a long time. Then he replied: 'Your question «Where is God?» asks that He be situated in space. But God was, with no location (*kāna 'Llah walā makān*); then, He created time and space, and He is now just as He was before both

ولا مكان» ، انتهى، أى لا وجود لهما فى ذاتهما فلا شىء معه، وفيها لا يزال. وسئل أبو الحسن النورى «أين الله من مخلوقاته ؟» قال «كان الله ولا أين والمخلوقات فى عدم فكان حيث هو وهو الآن حيث كان إذ لا أين ولا مكان» انتهى.

* نعوت الخمرة بعد التجلى

ولقد أرادت الخمرة أن تظهر محاسنها وتبرز أنوارها وأسرارها أظهرت قبضة من نورها حسية معنوية. فمن جهة حسها محدودة محصورة، ومن جهة معناها غير محدودة ولا محصورة، بل هى متصلة ببحر المعانى الذى لا نهاية له. فمثالها كثلجة فى بحر لا ساحل له، فالثلجة من جهة جمودها محصورة، ومن جهة مائها الباطنى متصلة بالبحر الذى هى فيه، فنسبة القبضة من جهة حسها ببحر المعانى الباقى على لطافته، كنقطة فى بحر أو كخردلة فى الهواء[٣]، والحاصل أن القبضة التى ظهرت فى بحر المعانى هى عين البحر الذى ظهرت منه، وأسرار الربوبية مجموعة فيها ثم اختصرت فى الآدمى ولذلك قال بعضهم

time and space'. Time and space have no existence in themselves, and there is nothing with Him in eternity that has either a beginning or an end.

Someone asked Abū'l-Hasan al-Nūrī:[7] 'Where was God relative to His creatures?' He replied: 'God was, without any where, and the creatures [were] in nothingness (*fī ʿadam*); He was in Himself (*haythu huwa*) and He is now just as He was (*haythu kān*), for there is neither where, nor location.'

On the Characteristics of the Essence After the Theophanic Radiation

When the Essence wanted its beautiful qualities (*mahāsin*) to become apparent and its lights and secrets to be made manifest, it had a 'Handful' (*qabḍa*) of its light appear in a fashion that was both sensible and spiritual. Seen from its sensible manifestation, it (this cosmic 'first matter') appears to be limited and finite, while seen from its spiritual manifestation, it is neither limited nor finite, but rather united to the Ocean of Divine Ideas (*baḥr al-maʿānī*), which is infinite. It may be compared to a block of ice that is dipped into a boundless ocean. If the ice is looked at as an inert block, it is finite; if it is looked at relative to the water that constitutes its inner nature, it is united with the sea in which it is submerged. The relationship between the Handful, looked at from its sensible aspect, and the Ocean of Divine Ideas, whose subtle (*laṭāfa*) nature is immutable, is similar to that of the drop and the ocean, or to that of the grain of pollen and the air through which it floats. Consequently, the Handful appearing within the Ocean of Divine Ideas is indistinguishable from the Ocean itself, from which it originates. The secrets of Lordship (*asrār al-rubūbiyya*) are gathered together in the Handful, and then summed up in the human being (*al-ādamī*). This is why the poet sang [meter *kāmil, hā'iyya*]:

يا تائها في مهمه عن سرّه ❁ انظر تجد فيك الوجود بأسره
أنت الكمال طريقة وحقيقة ❁ يا جامعا سر الإله بأسره

وقال فى المباحث

اعقل فأنت نسخة الوجود ❁ لله ما أعلاك من موجود
أليس فيك العرش والكرسى ❁ والعالم العلوى والسفلى

وإحاطة بحر المعانى بالعرش واستيلاؤه عليه هو معنى الاستواء الذى وقع فى القرآن عند المحققين، وإلى ذلك أشار ابن عطاء الله فى الحِكَم بقوله «يا من استوى برحمانيته على عرشه فصار العرش غيبا فى رحمانيته كما صارت العوالم غيبا فى عرشه، محقتَ الآثار بالآثار ومحوتَ الأغيار بمحيطات أفلاك الأنوار» فالقبضة التى ظهرت من بحر الجبروت هى صورة العرش وما احتوى عليه من العوالم وقد استولت عليه أسرار المعانى التى لا نهاية لها وأحاطت به من كل جانب حتى صار العرش غيبا أى شيئا تافها لا نسبة له فى جانب تلك الأسرار، كما صارت العوالم التى فى جوف العرش غيبا فى وجود العرش، إذ

O you who wander through the desert, your secret lost,
Look! All existence may be found within you.
You are perfection, in act and in truth,[8]
O you who bring together the entire Divine Secret.

The author of the *Mabāhith*[9] wrote:

Consider this: you are the ideal sum of existence,
By God, how sublime a being you are!
Are both Throne and Footstool not within you,[10]
Both the upper world and the lower?

The Ocean of Divine Ideas surrounds the Divine Throne and dominates it: this is what the Qurʾānic expression (7:53, and passim) means: 'God is seated [on the Throne]', according to the interpretation offered by those who truly know. This is also what Ibn ʿAṭāʾ Allāh was referring to in his *Ḥikam,* when he said: 'Oh you who are seated upon your Throne with your Mercy: through your Mercy you have both made the Throne invisible and hidden the worlds in your Throne. You have wiped away all traces with traces, and you have absorbed all otherness in the infinity of the luminous spheres.'

The Handful that appears in the Ocean of Omnipotence (*baḥr al-jabarūt*) is the image (*sūra*) of the Throne and of all the worlds it contains. But the secrets of the Divine Ideas, which are endless, dominate the Throne and surround it on all sides such that the Throne disappears or, in other words, that it becomes a thing of little importance or worth relative to the secrets, just as the worlds contained within the throne are wiped away in the presence of the Throne, with which they have a relationship analogous to that of a circle (drawn in the sand) in the desert (wherein this circle is drawn).

نسبتها معه كحلقة في فلاة. فالرحمانية وصف للذات والصفة لا تفارق الموصوف فكنى بالرحمانية عن أسرار الذات وهي المعاني الخارجة عن القبضة التي لا نهاية لها وهي التي أحاطت بالعرش من فوقه ومن تحته ومن كل جانب حتى صار غيبا فيها.

وقوله «محقت الآثار بالآثار» أي محقت الأكوان التي في جوف العرش بالعرش، وقوله «ومحوت الأغيار بمحيطات أفلاك الأنوار» أي محوت وجود العرش وما احتوى عليه بالأنوار المحيطات به، حتى انمحى اسمه ورسمه، وما بقي إلا وجود الأنوار المتدفقة من بحر الأسرار، وفي بعض الأخبار «والذي نفسي بيده لو ادَّلَّى أحدكم بحبل لوقع على الله»، أي على عظمة الله» كما لو عُرِّج بأحدكم إلى ما فوق العرش لوقع على عظمة الله» اه بمعناه. وفي بعض الآثار أن ملكا أراد أن يطير في الهواء، من فوق العرش فاستأذن ربه فأذن له وقواه بقوة ثلاثين ألف ملك، فطار ثلاثين ألف سنة، فقال يا رب أين أنت؟ فقال أنا معك، ثم طار ثلاثين أخرى فقال يارب أين أنت؟ فقال أنا معك، ثم طار ثلاثين كذلك، فقال أين أنت؟ فقال معك، فقال سبحانك ما أعظم شأنك. فطلب أن يرده إلى مكانه فرده، أو كما قال، يتحصل أن نسبة العرش من بحر المعاني المحيط

Mercy is a quality of the Essence, and this quality is inseparable from that which is qualified. The word 'Mercy' (used in Ibn ʿAṭāʾ Allāh's sentence) is a metonymy for 'the secrets of the Essence', meaning the Divine Ideas that come out of the Handful, are infinite, and completely encompass the Throne: above, below, and on all sides, to the point where it disappears in them.

The words 'You have wiped away all traces with (other) traces' mean: 'You have erased beings, which are contained within the Throne, by means of the Throne.' And the words: 'You have resolved alterity in the infinity of celestial lights' mean: 'You have resolved the existence of both the Throne and what it comprises in the lights which encompass it, to the point that its name and its form have disappeared and nothing remains but the lights that shine forth from the Ocean of secrets.'

According to one traditional saying (*khabar*), the Prophet said: (this is at least the sense of his words, if not the precise words he uttered), 'If one of you allowed himself to be let down on a rope, he would fall upon God,' meaning, upon the Magnificence of God, 'and, likewise, if one of you were hoisted up above the Throne, he would reach God's Magnificence.'

Another saying reports that one of the angels wanted to fly off into the space located above the Throne. He asked his Lord for permission, which was granted, along with the strength of thirty thousand angels. He thus flew for thirty thousand years, whereupon he spoke to God, inquiring: 'So Lord, where are You?' 'I am with you', was the reply. The angel continued flying for an additional thirty thousand years, and then asked the same question, to which he received the same answer. He flew off a third time, for another thirty thousand years, and then asked the same question, to which he received the same reply. 'Glory be to You, whose Magnificence has no limit!' exclaimed the angel; then he begged the Lord to take

به كشىء تافه ولذلك تجد قلب العارف يتسع باعتبار الفكرة حتى يصير العرش والكرسى فى زاوية من قلبه[4] .

قال بعضهم «العرش والكرسى مُنْدَكَّانِ فى ترسى» وسبب اتساعه لهذا الأمر العظيم أن الفكرة إذا جالت فى العظمة الفوقية التى لا نهاية لها وفى العظمة التحتية والأولية والآخرية التى لا نهاية لكل واحدة منها، وأوسعت النظرة فى ذلك، بقى العرش معلقا فى العظمة كخردلة فى الهواء، فصار فى زاوية من زوايا القلب الذى جالت فكرته فى تلك العظمة .

وهذه القبضة، تسمى قبضة محمدية، لأن الله تعالى لما أراد أن يتجلَّى ليُعرف أظهر قبضة من نوره فقال لها «كونى محمدا» ، فتطورت على صورة محمد عليه السلام كما فى بعض الأحاديث . ومن هذه القبضة تفرعت الأكوان كلها، فهى بذرة الوجود «منها انشقت الأسرار وانفلقت الأنوار»، أسرار الذات، وأنوار الصفات، وتُسمى أيضا آدم الأكبر، لأنها تفرعت منها الأشباح والأرواح .

فظاهر هذه القبضة، حسها محمدى وباطنها معنى قدسى، ظاهرها شريعة وباطنها حقيقة ظاهرها مُلك وباطنها ملكوت،

him back to the original point of his departure, and it was done. This is how the angel received the knowledge that the Throne is a small thing relative to the Ocean of Divine Ideas that surrounds it. This is also the reason why you note that the heart of the gnostic expands during meditation,[11] such that the Throne and the Footstool occupy only a small corner of his heart.

Someone (a Sufi) said: 'The Throne and the Footstool have overflowed onto my shield.' The cause of this ineffable expansion comes from the fact that when meditation changes into the Magnificence from on high, which is infinite, and into Magnificence from below, into that which precedes (all manifestation) and that which comes at the end (of all manifestation) – both of which are infinite – and contemplation (*naẓra*) expands in this Magnificence, the Throne remains suspended in the Magnificence just as a pollen spore is in the air, constituting just one of the [countless] corners of the heart, since the heart, in its meditation, bathes in this Immensity.

The 'Handful' at issue here is called 'Muhammadan', since when God decided to reveal Himself so that He could be known, he fashioned a Handful of His Light and had it appear, saying to it: 'Be Muhammad!' As we know from certain *ḥadīths*, the Handful then took on the form of Muhammad (upon whom be peace!). All beings are derived from this Handful; it is the seed of existence. As the Sufi Ibn Mashīsh said: 'All secrets emanate from it, and from it do all lights radiate,'[12] meaning the secrets of the Essence and the lights of the Qualities. Another name for it is 'the great Adam' (*al-Adam al-Akbar*, the macrocosm), since both bodies (*ashbāḥ*) and spirits (*arwāḥ*) have their origin in it.

On the outside, this Handful is thus the sensible manifestation of Muhammad, while on the inside it is holy intelligibility. Its outer aspect is religious law (*sharīʿa*), and its inner aspect is spiritual reality (*ḥaqīqa*); its exterior is the Kingdom (*mulk*), its interior is Royalty

ومـا أحاط بها من بحر المعانى جبروت، فإذا رُدّت الفروع إلى أصلها صار الجميع جبروتا كما هو فى الحقيقة .

فالمعانى التى هى عالم الملكوت، لا يمكن إظهارها إلا فى مظاهر الحِسّىّ الذى هو عالـم المُلك . فما ظهرت أنوار الملكوت وبهجته وحسنه إلا فى عـالم المُـلك، فالملك رياض للملكوت، فيه ظهر جماله وحسن طلعته . فما تبهج الملكوت، وظهرت محاسنه إلا بزهر جمال مولانا محمد صلى الله عليه وسلم الذى ظهر فى عالم المُلك .

وكما تجلّى الحق جل جلاله فى هـذه القبضـة باسمه الظاهر تجلى فيها أيضا باسمـه الباطن، فأظهر فيها أوصاف العبودية بعد أن تجلى فيها بأسرار الربوبيـة فاجتمع فيها الضدان، ربوبية وعبوديـة، فالمظهر للربوبيـة والقالب للعبوديـة وكل ما تجلى منها بهذا الوصف .

فمن وقف مع ظاهر القوالب حجب عن أسرار الربوبية وكان جاهلا بالله . ومن نفـذ إلى شهود بواطن الأشياء، وجدهـا نورانية ملكوتية وكان عارفا بالله، ولذلك قـال فى الحِكم «الكون كله ظلمـة وإنما أناره ظهور الحق فيـه . فمن رأى الكون ولم يشهد الحق فيه أو قبله أو بعده أو معه فقد أعوزه وجود الأنوار

(*malakūt*), while the ocean of Divine Ideas that surrounds it on all sides is Omnipotence (*jabarūt*). If ramifications (everything that springs forth from the primordial Handful) are brought back to their origin, the whole becomes Omnipotence, just as it is in reality (from all eternity, as they allow themselves to be grasped as distinct entities only in order to allow the creatures to realise the divine wish 'to be known').

The Divine Ideas that constitute the world of Royalty can become apparent only in sensible substrates, constituting the world of the Kingdom. It is only here that the lights of Royalty allow their splendour and their beauty to be seen, such that the Kingdom (as the author of the *Mashīshiyya* said) is 'the garden of Royalty', wherein Royalty can show its beauty and the brilliance of its face. Likewise, Royalty only shines, and its marvellous qualities only appear, through the dazzling beauty of our master, Muhammad (may prayer and blessings be upon him!), who manifested himself in the world of the Kingdom.[13]

Just as the Absolute (*al-ḥaqq*) has revealed Himself in this Handful (the cosmic Muhammadan form, the Universal Man) via His Name 'the Outer', He has also revealed Himself by His Name 'the Inner'. After revealing Himself in the Handful through the secrets of Lordship, He caused the attributes of servitude to appear in it. Thus, the two opposing worlds (opposing, yet complementary to theophanic revelation), Lordship and servitude, are reunited in the Handful. The revealing form (*al-maẓhar*: the creature as a place of epiphany) is made to (allow the appearance of) the state of Lordship, while the individualized form (*al-qālab*, literally, the 'mould') is made for (the reception and manifestation of) the state of servitude and all that devolves from it.

Whoever stops at the outer appearance of the 'moulds' remains behind a veil that conceals the secrets of Lordship, and in a state of ignorance relative to God.

وحجبت عنه شموس المعارف بسُحب الآثار» وقال أيضا «سبحان من ستر سر الخصوصية بظهور وصف البشرية وظهر بعظمة الربوبية في إظهار العبودية»، وقال الشاعر

لقد ظهرت فما تخفى على أحد ❁ إلا على أكمه لا يبصر القمرا
لكن بطنت بما أظهرت محتجبا ❁ وكيف يعرف من بالعزة استترا

فتحصل أنَّ الحق جل جلاله تجلى بين الضدين، بين حِسٍّ ومعنى، بين ربوبية وعبودية، بين قدرة وحكمة، فالقدرة عبارة عن أسرار المعاني القائمة بالأواني والحكمة عبارة عما ظهر في الأواني، من تشكيل وتقييد وتخصيص، وما يلزمها من أوصاف البشرية وأحكام العبودية.

فالضدان موجودان في كل مظهر، فعالم القدرة حق ويسمى عالم الملكوت وعالم المعاني وعالم الأرواح، وهو محل ظهور كمالات الربوبية، وعالم الحكمة حق، ويسمى عالم الملك، وعالم الحس وعالم الأشباح، وهو محل ظهور نقائص العبودية أدبا مع حضرة الربوبية ولا نقص في الحقيقة ولذلك قال صاحب العينية

But he who manages to penetrate the vision of the inner aspect of things observes that they are of a luminous nature, that they belong to Royalty; he knows God.

This is what was behind the statement of the author of the *Ḥikam* when he said: 'The universe is but darkness, the manifestation of God in it is its only light. He who looks at the universe without seeing God in it, or before it, or after it, or with it, is deprived of the presence of lights, and the clouds of relativity (*āthār*) shield the suns of knowledge from him.' And, 'Glory be to Him who has put a cover upon the secret of specificity (absolute in its Essence: *al-khuṣūṣṣiyya*) by making apparent the attributes of human nature (*wasf al-bashariyya*), and who has brought out the magnificence of His lordly nature by making apparent the state of servitude.'

The poet said [the meter is *basīt, rāʿiyya*]:

You appeared, and you remain hidden to no one,
except to him who is blind from birth and cannot see the moon.
But you have hidden yourself by creating a veil
out of what you were showing;
How can one know Him who cloaks Himself in Almightiness?

The Absolute (exalted may He be) thus revealed Himself between two opposing modes: the sensible and the intelligible, Lordship and servitude, Power (*al-qudra*) and Wisdom (*al-ḥikma*). 'Power' is a term that refers to the spiritual secrets residing within receptacles, while the word 'Wisdom' applies to that which appears in the receptacles: formal determination, limitation and particularity, as well as human attributes and the laws that govern the state of servitude, which are the necessary corollaries of all formal manifestation.[14]

These two opposing worlds are present wherever manifestation takes place. The world of Power is real (*ḥaqq*); it is called 'the world

وكل قبيح إن نسبت لحسنه ❁ أتتك معاني الحسن فيه تسارع
يكمل نقصان القبيح جماله ❁ فما ثم نقصان ولا ثم باشع

والناس باعتبار شهود هذين الضدين على ثلاثة أقسام،

قسم لم يشهدوا إلا عالم الحكمة، وقفوا مع ظواهر الأشباح ولم يرتقوا إلى عالم الأوراح، وهم أهل الدليل والبرهان من عوام أهل اليمين،

وقسم لم يشهدوا إلاَّ عَالَمَ القدرة وهو عالم المعاني الذى هو عالم الملكوت نفذوا من شهود عالم الأشباح إلى عالم الأرواح، فغابت عنهم الأشكال والرسوم فى شهود أنوار الحى القيّوم، فلو كلفوا أن يشهدوا غيره لم يستطيعوا، وهم أهل الفناء فى الذات من المجذوبين المغرقين فى الأنوار، المطموس عنهم الآثار وهم القائلون

of Royalty', 'the world of intelligible realities' (or 'Divine Ideas'), or 'the world of spirits'; it is the place where the perfections of the state of Lordship are manifested. And the world of Wisdom is real; it is called 'the world of the Kingdom', 'the world of the senses', or 'the world of bodies'; it is the place where the imperfections of the state of servitude are manifested. If, in this latter case, one speaks of 'imperfections', it is only in deference to the state of Lordship; in reality, there is no imperfection. In this sense, the author of the *ʿAyniyya*[15] wrote [in *tawīl* meter]:

> *If you bring it back to its beauty, everything ugly*
> *Will immediately open beautiful meanings to you.*
> *The imperfection of the ugly is made perfect by its beauty:*
> *There, there is no imperfection, nor is there ugliness.*

Depending on the way they look upon these two opposing worlds, men fall into one of three categories:

(1) Those who see only the world of Wisdom, who stop at bodily appearances and make no progress toward the world of spirits. These are the people of demonstrations and proofs (*ahl al-dalīl wa'l-burhān*); they make up most of the 'people of the right'.[16]

(2) Those who see only the world of Power, that is, the world of intelligible realities, the world of Royalty: from the corporeal world they have penetrated into the world of spirits, such that formal and limited things are resolved for them (solely) in the vision of the lights of the Living One, He who subsists by Himself. If they were forced to contemplate anything other than Him, they would be incapable of doing so. These are the people of extinction in the Essence (*al-fanāʾ fī'l-dhāt*), who are ravished by ecstasy (*majdhūb*), plunged into the lights [of intelligible realities], in the eyes of anyone for whom the

فلم يبق إلا الله لم يبق كائن ❁ فما ثم موصول ولا ثم بائن
بذا جاء برهان العيان فما أرى ❁ بعينى إلا عينه إذ أعاين

وقسم أكمل منهم وهم الذين يشهدون القدرة فى محلها، والحكمة فى محلها مع اتحاد مظهرهما[6]، فيعطون القدرة حقها من الشهود والحكمة حقها من الأدب والتعظيم، فلم يحجبهم شهود القدرة عن الحكمة، ولا شهود الحكمة عن القدرة، فهم مجموعون فى فرقهم، مفروقون فى جمعهم، كلما شربوا ازدادوا صحوا وكلما غابوا ازدادوا حضورا، وهم أهل البقاء قد اتسعت دائرة معرفتهم، فتارة تصعد أرواحهم إلى محل الحرية، فيغرقون فى أنوار العظمة الربوبية، فتغيب عنهم الرسوم والأشكال، والرسوم[7] التى هى محل العبودية، وتارة تتنزل أرواحهم إلى محل العبودية فتتفنن فى علوم عالم الحكمة، وتتلذذ بحلاوة المناجاة[8] والتعلق مع الحبيب فى الخلوة، فهى تتنعم فى جنتين عن يمين وشمال، فيقال لها ولأربابها ﴿كلوا من رزق ربكم واشكروا له بلدة طيبة﴾ وهى جنة الجمع ﴿ورب غفور﴾ لنقائص جنة الفرق، والله تعالى أعلم.

traces (the world of formal manifestation) have been wiped away. It is they who say:

Only God remains; no being is left;
There, there is no connection, nor is there separation.
Of this I have visual proof, for through myself [= *my eye*]
I see only His Self when I look.[17]

(3) The third category reaches a higher degree of perfection than its predecessors. It is comprised of those who see Power in its place and Wisdom in its place, but they simultaneously see the unity of their place of manifestation. These individuals give Power its due by means of contemplation, and Wisdom its due by means of proper actions and pious veneration. The sight of Power is not a veil that hides Wisdom from them, any more than the sight of Wisdom veils Power from them. They are unified in their separation (meaning that, while perceiving the distinctive natures of beings and their reciprocal relationships, they intuitively recognize the ontological unity that underlies everything) and they are separate in their unification (meaning that their state of intimate union with Essential Reality does not keep them from grasping the existential 'traces' in their particularity, or from seeing the manifestation as distinct from the Principle, or the relative as distinct from the Absolute). When they drink (Wine, the Supreme Essence, the Holy Presence of which intoxicates ecstatics), their clarity increases [since they not only lose consciousness of their individual being, but also recognize the manifestation of the divine, both in themselves and in all things], and when they are ravished [that is, when they become absent to consciousness of objects that are normally perceived by the senses through being absorbed in contemplation of the one Essence], their presence is found to be increased [because they are no longer troubled

* خاتمة

سئل الولى العارف سيدى أحمد بن يوسف الملياني عن ذات الحق تعالى، هل هى حسية أو معنوية ؟ فأجاب بأنها حسية لا تدرك .

قلت وما قاله هو الحق لأن ذات الحق تعالى واجبة الوجود قائمة بنفسها متصفة بصفات المعانى والمعنوية والمعنى فى نفسها لا تقوم بنفسها ولا تتصف بصفات المعانى والمعنوية .

وتعبير بعض الصوفية عنها بالمعنى فى قولهم المعنى لا تظهر إلا بالحس والأوانى قائمة بالمعانى، فإنما ذلك مجرد اصطلاح عبروا عنها بالمعنى على وجه التشبيه والمجاز، وذلك أن ذات الحق تعالى لما كانت لطيفة خفية لا تدرك، أشبهت المعنى فى الخفاء فأطلقوا عليها معنى، ولا مشاحنة فى الاصطلاح كما اصطلحوا على إطلاق القدرة على الذات، والحكمة على الأثر وما يتعلق به من الأسباب والعلل وكما اصطلحوا على إطلاق الذات على ما ظهر من التجليات والصفات على ما يلزمها

by the vision of alterity, and they place themselves in the centre of what is essential, which is the intimate reality of each being].

These are 'the people of subsistence' (*ahl al-baqāʾ*). The circle of their knowledge (*maʿrifa*) has expanded so that sometimes their spirits rise up toward the place of freedom [absolute freedom, where they are united with the unconditioned source of existence] – then they bathe in the lights of the [infinite] Magnificence of Lordship, while formal and limited things that are subjected to the state of servitude disappear from their consciousness – and sometimes their spirits descend back toward the place of servitude [the conditions of manifested existence, where 'the servant remains the servant' and where even the highly developed saint continues to be subjected to the norms and properties that govern this state]. Their spirits then devote themselves to all the kinds of knowledge that pertain to the world of Wisdom; they taste both the sweetness of intimate conversation [with the Lord: *munājā*], and the bond that builds with the Beloved in retreat (*khalwa*); they enjoy the two gardens, that of the right, and that of the left (mentioned in the Qurʾān 34:15), and they are told: 'Eat what your Lord provides for you, and be thankful to Him, for that is a happy place' – a reference to the garden of union (*jannat al-jamʿ*) – 'and a forgiving Lord' – which is a reference to the imperfections of the garden of separateness (*jannat al-farq*), but God knows best!

Epilogue

Someone asked the holy gnostic Sīdī Ahmad b. Yūsuf al-Milyānī[18] about the Divine Essence (absolute reality: *dhāt al-ḥaqq*): 'Is it of an intelligible nature, or one that can be perceived by the senses?' His reply was : 'It is available to the senses, and it cannot be grasped!'

His answer was correct. Indeed, the Divine Essence exists

من التشكيلات والتخصيصات والتلوينات التي هي آثار الصفات إلى غير ذلك من اصطلاحاتهم نفعنا الله بجمعهم آمين.

وما أجاب به هذا السيد، هو تفسير للذات الأزلية حال الكنزية قبل التجلي، وأما بعد التجلي فهي حسية تدرك بواسطة التجليات الحسية، والجواب الجامع المطابق لاصطلاح المحققين من العارفين، أن يقول هي معنوية، تجلت في مظاهر القوالب الحسية، ونعني بالمعنوية اللطافة الأصلية، وقد قلت في رسمها، هي ذات قديمة أزلية لطيفة خفية متجلية بالرسوم والأشكال، متصفة بأوصاف الكمال، واحدة في الأزل وفيما لا يزال.

انتهى هذا آخر التقييد المبارك وصلى الله على سيدنا ومولانا محمد وآله وصحبه وسلم والحمد لله رب العالمين.

necessarily; it has in itself its sufficient reason; it is qualified by the Attributes of quality and qualification.[19] On the other hand, intelligible reality (*al-maʿnā*) [the Divine Ideas included in the Essence] does not have its sufficient reason in itself, and is not qualified by the Attributes of quality and qualification. If a Sufi should use the word *maʿnā* in reference to the Essence, as, for example, in maintaining that 'Essence is only manifested through that which can be perceived by the senses (*ḥiss*)' or that 'the receptacles (*awānī*) subsist through essences (*maʿānī*)', what is at issue is a purely conventional use of the term: the word *maʿnā* is used both analogically and metaphorically, since the Divine Essence, in that It remains both subtle and hidden, cannot be grasped: It thus resembles the intelligible reality (which underlies things and is) in a state of occultation. This comparison, which results from a technical convention, does not really lend itself to controversy.

Likewise, the Sufis have agreed to apply the word 'Power' (*al-qudra*) to the Essence, and the word 'Wisdom' (*al-ḥikma*) to the universe of formal 'traces' (*al-āthār*) and to both occasional and efficient causes (*al-asbāb wa'l-ʿilal*) connected to them.

Moreover, they have agreed to apply the term *dhāt* (meaning 'Essence' and thus, more generally, any 'thing in itself') to (the set of) manifestations, and the word *sifāt* (which initially refers to the Divine 'Qualities') to all formal determinations, specifications and modalities that are the necessary corollary to the 'traces' of Qualities. A number of other conventional expressions have been adopted in the same way by the Sufis – may God allow us to profit from their example!

The reply offered by Sīdī Ahmad b. Yūsuf is thus an explanation (*tafsīr*) that concerns the Eternal Essence in the state of non-manifestation, before theophanic revelation (since it is then 'ungraspable') and after theophanic revelation, since it takes on a

ملاحظات

١ فى الأصل «ظهر» والصواب «ظهرت».

٢ فى الأصل «عمى» والصواب «عماء».

٣ فى الأصل «الهوى» والصواب «الهواء».

٤ فى الأصل «قبله» والصواب «قلبه».

٥ فى الأصل «هذا» والصواب «هذين».

٦ فى الأصل «مظهرها» والصواب «مظهرهما».

٧ كذا فى الأصل ولعله خطأ من الناسخ لأنه مكرر.

٨ فى الأصل «المناجات».

modality of the senses, and can be grasped by means of manifestations of a sensible nature.

The general response corresponding to the expression normally used by accomplished gnostics entails saying that the Essence is of an intelligible nature (*maʿnawiyya*) and that it revealed itself in the substrates of differentiated, sensible forms. 'Intelligible nature' should be understood in the sense of original subtlety (*al-laṭāfa al-aṣliyya*). To describe its characteristics, I will say that it is Eternal Essence, without beginning or end, that it is subtle, hidden, manifested in formal, limited things, qualified by the attributes of perfection, and unique in both pre-eternity and in that eternity which has no end.

This treatise thus reaches its end: may it be a sign of divine grace! And may the Peace and Blessings of God be upon our lord and master Muhammad and his family and companions. Glory to God, Lord of the Worlds!

NOTES

1 *al-khamrat al-azaliyya*: on wine used as a symbol for the Divine Essence and the intoxication it gives rise to in the mystic's heart, see E. Dermenghem, *l'Eloge du Vin* (translation of Ibn al-Fāriḍ's *Khamriyya*) Paris, 1931, pp. 121–124.

2 *al-adhwāq al-salīma*: literally, the word *dhawq* means 'taste' (the *gustus* of the Church Fathers); it refers to direct, intuitive contact with spiritual reality, as opposed to access via the process of 'ratiocination'.

3 *ḥāl al-kanziyya,* literally 'the state of (hidden) treasure'. This expression comes from the *ḥadīth qudsī* in which God, speaking through the Prophet, states: 'I was a hidden treasure; but I longed to be known, and I created the creatures.'

4 Although past tense in Arabic, *kāna* is here translated as a present tense verb; no tense – meaning no 'time' – is really adequate, since the nature of the Essence is not in any way 'located' in duration: it was, is, and always will be identical to itself. All it does 'after' theophanic revelation (which is a process renewed at every single instant rather than one having continuity in time, as we shall see), is to shed light upon the latent possibilities that are contained in it for all eternity.

5 *Laṭāfa,* a noun derived from the Divine Name *al-Laṭīf,* meaning 'He who penetrates all things.' *Laṭāfa* is the redemptive quality of the Essence that manifests itself in informal existence, on the level of Divine Ideas (*maʿāni*), and stands in opposition to the opacity (*Kathāfa*) of gross (*al-kathīf*) manifestation that is perceptible to the senses.

6 This is a technical term that applies to mystical realisation; it suggests a change in state that 'travellers' (*sālikūn*) undergo as they progress through the successive stages of the mystical journey, in contrast to the stability (*tamkīn*) associated with beings who have 'arrived' (*wāṣilūn*) at the point of perfect gnosis, immersion in the Eternal Light.

7 A Baghdad Sufi who died in 295/907. He was a friend of Junayd and, like him, a follower of Sarī al-Saqatī.

8 *tarīqatan wa ḥaqīqatan,* literally: according to the (Sufi) path, and according to (spiritual) Reality.

9 *Al-Mabāḥith al-aṣliyya* ('fundamental research', a poem written in *rajaz* dealing with conditions and aspects of the Sufi Path, composed by Ibn al-Bannā al-Tujībī, a native of Saragosa who died in Fez in 821/1419

(according to Massignon, *Bibliographie hallajienne,* no. 600). These lines of poetry and Ibn ʿAjība's commentary – where he develops the doctrine of the analogy between the microcosm and the macrocosm – can be found on pp. 212–222 of volume II in the Cairo edition (1331/1913), which contains both *Al-Futūḥāt al-ilāhiyya fī sharḥ al-Mabāḥith al-aṣliyya* and *Iqāẓ al-himam fī sharḥ al-Ḥikam* (another commentary by Ibn ʿAjība, on Ibn ʿAṭāʾ Allāh al-Iskandarī's *Ḥikam*).

10 *al-ʿarsh wa'l-kursī*: these are the first two determinations that appear within the Primordial 'Handful'. The 'Throne' is analogous to the Universal Spirit (*al-Rūh*), which is also called the 'First Intellect' (*al-ʿaql al-awwal*), and the 'Footstool' to the Universal Soul (*nafs al-kull*).

11 *al-fikra*: contemplative, or illuminative, meditation, which should be distinguished from meditation as an exercise of thought (*tafakkur*); the former is an inborn faculty situated in the heart, and it spontaneously radiates out when the heart is freed from the veils of passion and cosmic illusion.

12 A quote from the *Mashīshiyya,* or *Tasliya Ibn Mashīsh,* a litany in praise of the Prophet composed by ʿAbd al-Salām Ibn Mashīsh, the teacher of Abū'l-Hasan al-Shādhilī (d. 625/1228). His tomb is located on Djebel ʿAlam, in the Rif, and is one of the holiest of Morocco's pilgrimage destinations. A French translation of the *Mashīshiyya*, with commentary, was published by T. Burckhardt in *Etudes traditionnelles* no. 3, Paris, Jan–Feb 1967.

13 This passage is a paraphrase from the *Mashīshiyya* (see the previous note) from which the image of the 'garden of Royalty…' was borrowed literally.

14 In contrast to certain other Sufis – like Ibn ʿArabī and the Ishrāqiyyūn – Ibn ʿAjība does not use the word *ḥikma* (Wisdom) in the sense of eternal Divine Wisdom (*theosophia*), accessible only to gnostics; rather – as was the case for Ghazālī (e.g., *Iḥyāʾ*, III, 47) – he used it to refer to cosmic harmony, the domain of laws (*aḥkām*), of ordinary causality (*alʿada*), upon which the distinctive and speculative knowledge of exoteric practitioners was practised. In a sense, it is the reign of divine immanence to which reason allows one to conform. *Qudra* (power), on the other hand, represents the vertical, transcendent divine dimension accessible only to the intuition (*basīra, fikra*) of the esotericists; it is *qudra* that, in the cosmic order, comes along to shatter the order of habitual causes and to produce what we call the 'miracle' (*muʿjiza, karāma*).

15 ʿAbd al-Karīm al-Jīlī, a Sufi born in Jīl (near Baghdad) in 767/1366, who died around 820/1408. Ibn ʿAjība is believed to have written a commentary on the poem.

16 According to the Qurʾān [56:8, 38–40], the Companions of the right are the blessed souls of Paradise, who comprise the 'multitude' of believers, among the first as well as the last of generations.

17 The alliteration cannot be translated here because of the double meaning of the word *ʿayn*: essence (being in itself, whence 'myself' and 'Himself') and eye: *mā arā biʿaynayya illā ʿaynahu idh uʿāyinu.*

18 A Sufi master in the *Shādhiliyya* order (d. 931/1524–25, in Miliana, Algeria). His followers, of which there are still a considerable number in the upper Moulouya River region in Morocco, are referred to as *Yūsufiyya,* or *Rashīdiyya* (cf. L. Rinn, *Marabouts et Khouans,* Algiers, 1884, pp. 272–273). He was the teacher of Aḥmad b. Mūsā al-Ḥasanī Mawlāy Karzāz (d. 1608), who founded the *Karzāziyya* brotherhood (ibid., ch. XXIII).

19 *Sifāt al-maʿānī wa'l-maʿnawiyya*: the seven 'positive' Divine Qualities that characterize the Essence, not in itself (like necessary Being or Unity), but according to a certain relationship with manifestation: Power, Will, Omniscience, Life, Hearing, Sight, and Speech, and the seven qualifiers that devolve from them, meaning the fact, for God, of being Powerful, Wilful, Omniscient, Living, Hearing, Seeing, and Speaking.

II

التقييد الثاني

* وله أيضا رضى الله عنه فى بيان الطلاسم التى احتجب بها عن الربوبية .

وبعد، فهذا تقييد عجيب يرفع حجاب الوهم عن الحاذق اللبيب يتضمن رفع الحجب عن السر المصون، و زوال الطلاسم عن الكنز المكنون، وسميته كشف النقاب عن سر لب الألباب وهذا أوله والله المستعان .

اعلم أن الحق جلّ جلاله أودع هذا الآدمى أسرار ذاته وصفاته وأفعاله، لكن حجب ذلك عنه بحكمته وقهره، فجعل على كل واحد من الأسرار الثلاثة طلسما، وحجابا مستورا فستر ذلك السر عن العبد بسبب الطلسم الذى غشى به قلبه .

* طلسم توحيد الأفعال

اعلم أن فعل العبد كله من الله، بأن لا فاعل فى الوجود سواه . قال تعالى ﴿ وربك يخلق مايشاء ويختار ماكان لهم الخيرة ﴾ وقال تعالى ﴿ إن ربك فعال لما يريد ﴾ وقال

The Talismans[1] that Veil the State of Lordship: Explanation

The aim of the marvellous overview that follows is to lift the veil of illusion (*wahm*) from the individual whose intelligence is keen. It deals with the lifting of the veils that cover the well-guarded secret, and with the disappearance of the talismans that protect the Hidden Treasure. I have called it 'the Unveiling of the Quintessential Secret' (*Kashf al-niqāb ʿan sirri lubbi al-albāb*).[2] It begins thus, and all assistance comes from God:

Know that God (the Absolute, the True: *al-ḥaqq*) – glory be to Him! – has deposited in man (*al-adamī*) the secrets of His Essence, of His Qualities, and of His Acts, but that, through His Wisdom and His Sovereign Dominance (*qahr*), He has veiled from him the knowledge of what He has deposited. He deposited a talisman, and stretched a veil over each of these three secrets such that the servant is unable to see the secret, because of the talisman covering his heart.

The Talisman of the Unity of Action

Know that every one of the servant's actions comes from God, and that, in existence, there is no agent other than He. God said: 'And your Lord creates what He wishes, and chooses what is best for them' [Q. 28:68]; 'Verily, your Lord does as He wishes' [Q. 11:108]; 'God created both you and what you do' [Q. 37:96]; 'Had God so wished, they would not have slain one another, but God does as He wishes' [Q. 2:253].

God Most-High has nevertheless placed upon the servant's heart a talisman by which He has hidden from him the light of unity in actions. This talisman is free will (*ikhtiyār*), which God has conferred

تعالى ﴿ والله خلقكم وما تعملون ولو شاء الله ما اقتتلوا ولكن الله يفعل ما يريد ﴾ .

ثم إن الحق جل جلاله جعل على قلب العبد طلسما غشى به نور توحيد الأفعال، وهو ما جعل له من الاختيار فى الظاهر، فتوهم أنه مختار إن شاء فعل، وإن شاء ترك .

وهذا يحس به كل عاقل من نفسه حتى يفرق بين حركة الارتعاش وغيرها، ولذلك قيل فى الجبرية إنهم قوم بُله حيث لم يفرقوا بينهما، وهذا هو المسمى بالكسب عند أهل السنة وبالحكمة عند أهل الصوفية، فيقولون القدرة تبرز، والحكمة تستر، وبسبب هذا الاختيار جاءت الشرائع وعليه يترتب الحساب، من الثواب والعقاب . وفى حقيقة الأمر، لا فاعل إلا الله، لكن هذا سر من أسرار الألوهية أخفاه الله عن عبده، وجعل له اختيار فى الظاهر لتقوم به الحجة عليه ﴿ قل فلله الحجة البالغة ﴾ وهذا السر الذى ستره الله، لا يصح للعبد أن يحتج به لنفسه فيترك العمل أو يعمل بالمعاصى، لأن العمل مطلوب من ناحية الشريعة، وهى إنما تعلقت بالظواهر .

وهذا الطلسم يغلظ ويرق بقدر رقة الحجاب وكثافته، فإذا غلظ الحجاب كثر فى العبد التدبير والاختيار، حتى ربما يجزم

upon man externally (*fī'l-zāhir*), such that man is under the illusion of being able to choose, and imagines that, if he wishes, he can opt to perform, or not to perform, some action.

All men endowed with reason personally experience this sense of apparent freedom, as when they note the distinction between (unconscious) movement like the trembling of a hand, and other (so-called 'voluntary') actions; and if those who make claims for absolute determinism (*al-jabriyya*) have been called 'fools', it is because they have been incapable of distinguishing between these two different kinds of action. The words 'acquisition' (*kasb*) and 'wisdom' (*ḥikma*) used by the Sunnis and the Sufis respectively, refer to free will. In this regard, the latter say that 'Power manifests and Wisdom covers'. Religious laws are decreed as a function of this free will, and the final reckoning – both rewards and punishment – relies on it.

In reality, however, there is no agent but God: but this truth is one of the secrets of the divine nature, which God has hidden from His servant in outwardly granting him free will so that it constitutes an argument against the servant (who is disobedient, in the sense that the servant cannot argue based on the fact that he was acting under duress). 'Say: to God belongs definitive argument' [Q. 6:149]. This secret that God has covered with a veil cannot be invoked by the servant in his favour in order to avoid performing the acts that are prescribed and that conform to the law, or in order to commit acts of disobedience, since all these acts are governed by religious law, and this law specifically concerns outward actions.

This talisman grows either thicker or thinner, depending on whether the opacity of the veil increases or decreases. If the veil becomes thicker, both the servant's determination to rely on himself (*tadbīr*) and free will grow stronger to the point that he occasionally goes so far as to affirm categorically that he himself is the agent, free in his acts, just as the Muʿtazilites imagined. But if the talisman

أنه الفاعل المختار، كما توهمت المعتزلة[1] وإذا ضعف الطلسم ورق الحجاب، قل تدبيره واختياره وانعزل من حوله وقوته فإذا اتصل العبد بشيخ التربية عزله عن اختيار نفسه وأمره بتحكيمه على نفسه فى أموره كلها فيقف عند أمره ونهيه. فإذا حصل له الفهم عن الله، وصار يفقهه قلبه فى الأمور حكّم الله على نفسه، وانعزل عن تدبيره واختياره، وإذا وقع منه التدبير والاختيار كان بالله ومن الله وإلى الله محلولا فيه، يدبر وينظر ما يفعل الله. فحينئذ ينكسر عنه الطلسم من توحيد الأفعال، فيرى الأفعال كلها من الله ذوقا وكشفا لا علما فقط. فيدخل حينئذ فى السبعين ألفا الذين يدخلون الجنة بغير حساب إذ لم يبق له فعل يحاسب عليه، بخلاف غيره فإنه لكثافة حجابه ينسب الفعل لنفسه أو لغيره، وعلامته أنه ينقص رجاؤه عند وجود الزلل، ويقوى عند وجود العمل، ويغضب عند من آذاه مع أنه يعتقد أنه لا فاعل إلا الله، وإن العبد مجبور فى قالب الاختيار، لكن لا يكفى فى هذا مجرد العلم، ولا بد من الذوق الصريح كما تقدم.

وعن هذا الذوق عبر الجيلانى رضى الله عنه حيث قال

weakens, the veil becomes thinner, and the servant sees his feeling of being able to rely on his own strength and to act freely somewhat diminished, and he counts less and less on his own powers and his own strength. If he then puts himself under a Shaykh's direction, the Shaykh distances him from free will, and commands him to rely on his judgment in all matters, to hold to what he – the Shaykh – commands and forbids; and if God should grant this disciple understanding and intelligence of the heart, it is God Himself who takes him into His custody and shelters him from both individual and free will. If desire and free will then manifest themselves in him, the occurrence is due to something that God has done, something that comes from God, which goes toward God, and which resides in Him (*mahlūl fīh*).[3] He becomes disposed to act, after which he looks at what God is doing. It is then, the talisman that had been covering the unity of action shatters. He sees that all actions come from God, through both direct experience and direct intuition, not just by virtue of theoretical knowledge. From that moment on, he becomes one of the seventy thousand elect who enter Paradise without needing to give an account [of their actions],[4] for there is no action left for which he needs to account, in contrast to those who, because of the thickness of their veil, attribute responsibility for their actions either to themselves or to someone else. Those in this latter category are known because their hope wanes when they notice (that they are committing) a sin, or because it grows when they note a good act; they are also seen to become irritated with those who harm them, even if (in principle) they believe that there is no actor other than God and that the servant is constrained within the mould of free will. In this domain, theoretical knowledge alone does not suffice; authentic experience is also needed, as we have just stated.

This is the experience that Al-Jaylānī[5] was referring to when he recited [two verses rhyming in *ʿayn, tawīl* meter]:

أراني كالآلات وهو محركي ❁ أنا قلم والاقتدار أصابعُ
ولست بجبري ولكن مُشاهد ❁ فِعالَ مريد ماله[2] من يُنازع

فإذا حصل للعبد هذا الذوق زال عنه الإشكال والتعارض بين الحقيقة والشريعة، فينزل الحقيقة في محلها وهو الباطن، والشريعة في محلها وهو الظاهر.

فقوله صلى الله عليه وسلم «اعملوا كل ميسر لما خلق له»، جمع فيه بين شريعة وحقيقة، فقوله «اعملوا» شريعة و «كل ميسر لما خلق له» حقيقة، فكأنه قال عليه السلام «اعملوا» أي توجهوا للعمل في الظاهر ولستم بعاملين في الحقيقة.

وقوله عليه السلام «لن يدخل أحدكم الجنة بعمله» حقيقة وقوله تعالى ﴿ادخلوا الجنة بما كنتم تعملون﴾ شريعة.

فالشريعة تنسب العمل للعبد باعتبار ما جعل فيه من الاختيار في الظاهر الذي هو الكسب، والحقيقة تنفيه عنه باعتبار ما في نفس الأمر.

وهكذا يسير العبد بين حقيقة وشريعة، فالحقيقة اعتقاد في الباطن، والشريعة عمل في الظاهر، وقد تمسك الكفار بالحقيقة

I see myself as the instrument, and it is He who moves me;
I am the pen in the hand of destiny.
In no way am I deterministic, but, as He acts,
I do watch Him whose will knows no opponent.

When the servant has had this experience, both doubts and opposition between spiritual reality (*al-ḥaqīqa*) and religious law (*al-sharīʿa*) begin to disappear for him; he puts spiritual reality in the place where it belongs, which is the esoteric domain (*al-bāṭin,* in one's heart of hearts), and religious law in its proper place, which is the exoteric domain (*al-zāhir,* the level of outer action).

The saying of the Prophet: 'Act! Each man will find ease in accomplishing that for which he was created,'[6] contains a synthesis of religious law and spiritual reality. The word 'act' actually refers to religious law, while the words 'each man will find ease, etc.' refer to spiritual reality. It is as if the Prophet were saying that we must direct ourselves zealously toward (virtuous) action in our outer lives, but that in reality it is not we who are acting.

Similarly, when the Prophet said: 'No one among us will enter Paradise because of his actions', he was expressing spiritual reality, while the divine words: 'Enter Paradise by virtue of what you have accomplished' [Q. 16:32] are referring to religious law.

Religious law thus attributes action to the servant, in consideration of the free will that has been given to him at the outer level: this is (the doctrine of) acquisition (of merit) (*kasb*). Spiritual reality (on the other hand) denies the servant's authorship of his acts, in consideration of the intrinsic truth of things.

The servant thus stands between spiritual reality and religious law, spiritual reality being the belief (that resides) in the innermost heart, and religious law being action (accomplished) outwardly. Misbelievers (*kuffār*) are characterised by their wishing to rely exclusively on inner

وحدها حيث قالوا ﴿ ولو شاء الله ما أشركنا ﴾، ﴿ ولو شاء الله ما عبدناهم ﴾ فلم ينفعهم ذلك حيث أهملوا الشريعة ورفضوها، وكذلك من قال «دعاني وسد الباب فما تكون حيلتي» فإنه احتج بالقدر مع أن الاختيار الذي جعله الله في العبد في الظاهر حاصل له في العادة، لأنه قادر على الخروج من الكفر بنطق الشهادة مثلا.

وأما الجبر الباطني، والقهر الإلهي، فلا يتعلق به التكليف إذ ليس في طوق العبد، بل هو من أسرار قهر الربوبية الذي اختص الله به ﴿ لا يسأل عما يفعل وهم يسألون ﴾.

قال سهل رضي الله عنه «للألوهية أسرار لو كشفت لبطلت النبوءات، وللنبوءات أسرار لو كشفت لبطل العلم، وللعلم أسرار لو كشفت لبطلت الأحكام» انتهى.

فلو انكشفت أسرار الألوهية من غير رداء لصار الخلق كلهم أغنياء عن تلقي العلم لاستغراقهم في بحار الأحدية، فلا يحتاجون إلى واسطة، ولو انكشفت أسرار النبوءات للخلق لصاروا كلهم علماء لظهور العلم الإلهي الذي كان كامنا في بطونهم، فيستغنون عن تلقي العلم من الأنبياء، ولو انكشفت أسرار العلم بحيث يتبين الشقي من السعيد لبطلت الأحكام، إذ يقول الشقي «لا ينفعني

reality in saying: 'Had God so wished, we would have associated none with Him' [Q. 6:148], or 'If God had wanted, we would not have worshipped them' [Q. 43:20]. But such claims will be of no use to them, because they neglect religious law and reject it, like the man who says: 'he called me and then shut the door; what am I supposed to do?' This is an argument based on predestination, while the same man would habitually[7] be capable of exercising free will – which God has conferred upon the servant – on the outer level, and he would thus have the power to leave his mistaken beliefs behind by, for example, choosing to pronounce the testimony of faith.

As for Divine Omnipotence, the constraining Sovereignty (*al-jabr*) that reigns over the level of intrinsic reality (*al-bāṭin*), is in no way concerned with (the servant's) responsibility, since it lies beyond the servant's reach and is one of the secrets of Lordly Power that belongs to God alone, as in the saying 'He will not be questioned about what He does, but they will be questioned' [Q. 21:23].

Sahl[8] said: 'To Divinity belong secrets which, if they were revealed, would render vain the missions of the prophets; to the missions of the prophets belong secrets which, if they were revealed, would render religious knowledge (*al-ʿilm*) vain; to religious knowledge belong secrets which, if they were revealed, would render legal prescriptions (*aḥkām*) vain.'

Indeed, if Divinity's secrets were made manifest with no veil whatsoever, there would be no need to transmit knowledge to men, so immersed would they be in the Ocean of Essential Unity (*al-aḥadiyya*), and, like the prophets, they would have no need of an intermediary (*al-wāsita*). If the secrets of the prophetic missions were revealed to them, men would all be knowers, since the divine knowledge hidden within their innermost hearts would shine forth in the light of day, and they would have no need of prophets to pass on such knowledge. And if the secrets of religious knowledge,

عمل» فلا يعمل، ويقول السعيد «أنا سعيد لا أحتاج إلى عمل» فتبطل أحكام الشرائع، فأبهم الله هذا الأمر عن عباده ودعا الكل إلى طاعته وتوحيده، فهدى من سبقت له السعادة، وخذل من سبق له الشقاء.

قال تعالى ﴿ والله يدعو إلى دار السلام ويهدي من يشاء إلى صراط مستقيم ﴾. ومن سبقت له رتبة عالية، حركه إلى النهوض لأسبابها. «إذا أراد الله أن يظهر فضله عليك خلق فيك ونسب إليك». ومن سبقت له رتبة متوسطة حركه إلى أسبابها على ما جرى به القدر السابق. فلا يصح الاحتجاج بالقدر في هذه الدار، فإن قلت قد[3] ورد في الحديث، أن آدم وموسى عليهما السلام قد تحاجا فقال موسى عليه السلام لآدم «أنت الذي خيبتنا وأخرجتنا من الجنة» وقال آدم «يا موسى أتلومني على أمر قضاه الله عليّ قبل أن أخلق» فحج آدم موسى أي غلبه بالحجة.

قلنا كان هذا الاحتجاج بعد موتهما في دار البرزخ وليست دار تكليف، وإنما هي دار التعريف فيصح الاحتجاج فيها بالقدر. وإن قلت كيف يتوجه العتاب إلى العبد وهو لم يفعل شيئا في الحقيقة، قلنا توجه إليه باعتبار نسبة الفعل لنفسه : على الاختيار

through which the difference between those who are wretched and those who are blessed becomes evident, were revealed to everyone, legal prescriptions would be offered to no avail; the wretched would say 'What good is there in acting?' and would do nothing, while the blessed would say 'I have all I ever wished for! I have no need to act'; in such cases, the precepts of religious law would lose all value. This is why God wanted this question to remain ambiguous for His servants, and He called all of them to be obedient to Him and to declare His Unity (*tawḥīd*), guiding those for whom blessedness was predestined, and leaving behind those who were destined for misfortune.

God said: 'God calls to the House of Peace, and guides whomever He wishes toward the straight path' [Q. 10:25]. He who was predestined to a high level is moved by God such that he hurries to seek the means to reach this elevation: 'If He wants to show His Grace to you, He will create (acts) in you, and will attribute (their merit) to you.'[9] He who was predestined to an intermediate level is pushed by God toward the means to reach it, in line with what was decreed from all eternity.

Using the argument of predestination (in order to abdicate one's responsibility) is not really appropriate in this world. If you look at the *ḥadīth*[10] in which Adam and Moses were arguing about predestination (Moses said, 'It is you who got us lost and caused us to depart from paradise', to which Adam retorted, 'Moses, are you blaming me for something God decreed for me to do even before I was created?' thus putting an end to the discussion), I would say that the discussion took place after the death of its two participants, in the intermediate world (*dār al-barzakh*), which is not the world of responsibility (*dār al-taklīf*) but rather the world of awareness (*dār al-taʿrīf*); in the latter world, it is appropriate to argue about predestination.

And if you say, 'What should we say when a servant is being blamed for something, when, in reality, it is not he who is acting?'

الذى خلقه الله فيه فى الظاهر. روى أن العبد إذا بلغ حد التكليف أرسل الله له ملائكة فيقولون له «من أنت ؟» فيقول «عبد الله». فيشهدون عليه بالعبودية لله. فإذا تحرك أول حركة قيل له «من فعل هذا ؟» فيقول «أنا». فيشهدون عليه بنسبة الفعل لنفسه. فعلى هذه النسبة يقع الحساب، فمن خرج عنها ذوقا وكشفا ورءاها من الله حقا سقط عليه الحساب كما تقدم فى السبعين ألفا والله تعالى أعلم.

* طلسم توحيد الصفات

اعلم أن هذا الهيكل الإنسانى جعله الله نموذجا ربانيا تحاكى صفاته صفات الرحمن، فجعل فيه قدرة وإرادة وعلما وحياة وسمعا وبصرا وكلاما وهذا معنى الحديث «إن الله خلق آدم على صورته» على بعض التأويلات لأن هذه الصفات التى جعلها الله فيه حادثة ناقصة وصفات الحق تعالى قديمة كاملة وهى كامنة فى الإنسان كمون الثمار فى الأغصان أو كمون الزبد فى اللبن فأصبحت صفات الحق القديمة بصفات العبد الحادثة. وقد تُخرَق له العادة فيظهر عليه من العلم، والقدرة أو السمع أو البصر أو الكلام ما

I would reply that if he is the one who is being reprimanded, it is because he is taking responsibility for his acts by virtue of the free will that God created in him at the outer level.

It is reported that when the servant reaches the age of reason, God sends angels to him to ask: 'Who are you?' He answers: 'God's servant' (*ʿabd Allāh*), and they become witnesses to his acts of servitude toward God. The next time he moves, they ask: 'Who just moved?' 'I did,' he replies, and they witness the fact that he is attributing his action to himself. The final reckoning will be based on this attribution; anyone who, by intuition and mystical unveiling, frees himself of this attribution and sees that in reality it belongs to God, finds himself simultaneously exempted from the reckoning, as we saw earlier in regard to the seventy thousand elect. But God is more knowing!

The Talisman of the Unity of Attributes

Know that God fashioned this human form (*al-haykal al-insānī*) as a lordly model whose attributes are in the likeness (*tuhākī*) of His own Attributes, the Attributes of the All-Merciful (*al-Raḥmān*); in it, He placed power, will, knowledge, life, hearing, sight and speech. According to several commentators, this is the meaning of the *ḥadīth*: 'God created Adam in His likeness.'

Nevertheless, the attributes that God placed in man are contingent and imperfect, while Divine Attributes are eternal and perfect. They are hidden in man, as fruit is among branches or as butter is in milk. In other words, God's Eternal Attributes are veiled by the contingent attributes of the servant. And even if through some extraordinary intervention[11] it occasionally happens that man exhibits stupendous knowledge and power, or an ability to hear, see, or speak that dazzles the understanding, (this is nothing but a fleeting manifestation upon

يبهر العقول ثم يستر ذلك عنه فيرجع لأصله ويقف عند حده.
فلما احتجبت عنه صفات الحق بطلسم وجود صفات نفسه، زعم أنه يقدر بقدرته ويريد بإرادته ويحيى بحياته ويسمع بسمعه ويبصر ببصره ويتكلم بكلامه، وفى الحقيقة إنما صفاته قائمة بصفات الحق وشعاع من شعاعها لا تأثير لها أصلا. فإذا انكسر عنه هذا الطلسم الوهمى وارتفع له الحجاب عن توحيد الصفات تحقق ألا قدرة له ولا إرادة ولا علم ولا حياة إلا بقدرة الله وإرادته، وكذا سائر صفاته، فصار يتحرك بقدرة الله، ويريد بإرادته، ويسمع ويبصر بالله، ويتكلم بالله، وفى ذلك يقول الششترى رضى الله عنه «أنا بالله أنطق، ومن الله أسمع»، وقول القطب ابن مشيش «حتى لا أرى ولا أسمع ولا أحس ولا أجد إلا بها». وفى مثل هذا ورد الحديث «فإذا أحببته كنت سمعه الذى يسمع به وبصره الذى يبصر به» الحديث والله تعالى أعلم.

* طلسم توحيد الذات

اعلم أن الله تعالى كان كنزا خفيا لطيفا أزليا لم يعرفه أحد.
فلما أراد أن يُعرف تجلى بتجليات من ذلك الكنز كتمها وأظهرها

which) a veil is then stretched, and the man returns to his initial state and remains within the limits appropriate to him.

As long as the Divine Attributes remain veiled by the talisman of his own attributes, man can pretend to act with his own power, or to want with his own will, or to live with his own life, to hear with his own sense of hearing, or to see with his own sight, or to use language through his own power of speech. In reality, his attributes are completely dependent on the Divine Attributes; they are rays coming from Their rays; (in themselves) they have no influence (*ta'thīr*) whatsoever. But if this illusory talisman should rip and the veil that hides the unity of attributes from him should be lifted, he then realises that he has neither power nor will, neither knowledge nor life, except through the Power and the Will, and through all the Divine Attributes; from that moment on, he moves through God's Power, he wants through God's Will, he sees and hears through God, and speaks through God.

Shustarī[12] wrote in this regard: 'It is through God that I speak, through Him that I hear.'

Likewise, the 'spiritual pole' (*quṭb*) Ibn Mashīsh expressed the following words on the same subject: '...Such that I cannot see, hear, feel, or exist, except through It.'[13]

This is also the meaning of the *ḥadīth* (in which God speaks through the Prophet's words, saying): 'And when I love [my servant], I am the ear with which he hears, the eye with which he sees,' etc. (see the complete text).[14] But God is more knowing!

The Talisman of the Unity of Essence

Know that God was a subtle, Hidden Treasure, existing from all eternity, whom no one knew. And when He yearned to be known, He revealed Himself through manifestations that radiated out of this state of non-manifestation, giving them both density and appearance,

بمقتضى اسمه الظاهر ثم أبطنها وسترها بمقتضى اسمه الباطن فصارت ظاهرة باطنة أبطنها بما أظهر عليها من أحكام العبودية وأوصاف البشرية ونعوت الحدثية من حسّ التكوين والتشكيل والتقييد والتحيز ولا حادث في الحقيقة إنما تجدد لها التجلي والظهور فبطنت بعد ظهورها فتحقق فيها اسمه الظاهر والباطن، فمن نظر إلى أصلها وغاب عن حسها لم يحتجب بها عن الحق ورآه ظاهرا فيها. ومن وقف مع حسها الظاهر حجب بها عن شهود الحق وصارت في حقه ظلمة، ولذلك قال في الحِكم «الكون كله ظلمة وإنما أناره ظهور الحق فيه» فإنما هو ظلمة في حق أهل الحجاب، وأما في حق أهل العيان فالكون عندهم كله نور. فإذا اتصل العبد بشيخ التربية، غيّبَهُ عن أوصاف بشريته بشهود روحانيته وعن أحكام العبودية، بظهور نور الربوبية وعن حس الكائنات بشهود معاني أسرار الذات، فيغيب عن نفسه بشهود محبوبه، وعن الكون بشهود المكون، ويقال مقام المحبوبية كما ورد في بعض روايات الحديث المتقدم. فإذا أحبته

in accord with His Name 'The Apparent' (*al-zāhir*); then He hid them and veiled them in accord with His Name 'The Hidden' (*al-bāṭin*). The manifestations thus became apparent-hidden, made hidden by the very thing that God made visible in them, meaning the laws of the state of servitude, the attributes of the human condition and the contingent characteristics of sensory manifestation: structure, form, limit and location. There is no contingency in reality, however, but rather a recurrent manifestation whose appearance is renewed, and then hidden again, such that the Divine Names 'The Apparent' and 'The Hidden' are actualized in it.

For whoever looks at manifestation at its very roots and avoids considering its sensory aspect, manifestation does not become a veil that hides God; rather, he sees God appearing in it. He who stops at the external, sensory aspect of manifestation, on the other hand, finds himself veiled from the sight of God; manifestation is nothing but darkness for him. It is for this reason that the author of the *Ḥikam* said 'The universe is but darkness; the manifestation of God in it is its only light.'

The universe is darkness only for the eyes of those who are veiled, however. For those whose vision is freed, the entire universe is light. If the servant attaches himself to a Shaykh for his teachings, the latter completely detaches him from the attributes of his human nature, by having him contemplate his spiritual (*rūḥāniyya*) nature; similarly, he detaches him both from the statutes of the state of servitude by making manifest for him the light of the state of Lordship, and from the sensory aspect of the created universe by having him see the meanings of the essential secrets. Man is thus made absent to himself thanks to the presence of his Beloved, absent to creation through the presence of the Creator. This is the state that is referred to in the expression 'the station of love' (*maqām al-maḥbūbiyya*), which comes from the version of the *ḥadīth* cited above 'And when I love him, I am him!'

كُنته، فإذا انكسر هذا الطلسم وهو وجود العبد الوهمى ووقوفه مع أوصاف بشريته بالغيبة عنها، ظهر له الكنز الذى كان خفيا، وهو الذات الأقدس، فيدخل مقام الإحسان، وينال رتبة الشهود والعيان، الوَلاية الكبرى والسعادة العظمى، وعن هذا عبر ابن العريف رضى الله عنه .

بدا لك سر طال عنك اكتتامه ❁ ولاح صباح كنت أنت ظلامه
فأنت حجاب القلب عن سر غيبه ❁ ولولاك لم يطبع عليه ختامه
فإن غبت عنه حل فيه وطنبت ❁ على موكب[4] الكشف المصوب خيامه
وجاء حديث لا يُملُّ سماعه ❁ شهى إلينا نثره ونظامه
إذا سمعته[5] النفس طاب نعيمها ❁ وزال عن القلب المعنَّى غرامه

وقال الششترى فى بعض أزجاله

ياقاصداعين الخبر الخُبرُ ❁ غطاه أينك
الخُبرُ منك والخبر ❁ والسر عندك
ارجع لذاتك واعتبر ❁ ما ثم غيرك

When the talisman that is comprised of the servant's illusory existence and his attachment to attributes of his human condition is shattered by annihilating these attributes, the treasure that until then was hidden – the Most Holy Essence – appears to the servant, and the servant enters the station of excellence (*maqām al-iḥsān*), reaches the degree of contemplation and direct vision (*shuhūd wa ʿiyān*), of perfect sainthood, of supreme beatitude.

It was in regard to this station that Ibn Al-ʿArīf wrote [five verses, *tawīl*, rhyming in *ha'*]:

A secret, long hidden, was revealed to you;
Dawn broke, and you were its night.
'Tis you who veil the secret of its mystery from your heart:
Were it not for you, your heart would not be sealed.
Should you absent yourself from it, it becomes the campground
Wherein the caravan – bearer of the well-guarded illumination
– sets up its tents.
Inspired words are then heard, and hearkened tirelessly,
Their prose and verse fill us with zeal,
It brings joy to the hearer's soul
And wipes away the longing of the pining heart.' [15]

In one of his *zajals* Shustarī wrote:

O you in search of the real news,
Your conditioned existence covers it over.
News and its verification come from within you;
the secret is in you.
Come back to your essential being and look:
there is no one there but you.

ثم قال

اسمع كلامي والتهم ❁ إن كنت تفهم
لأن كنزك قد عدم ❁ عن كل طلسم

اعلم أن وجود هذا الطلسم حق، وحكمة صون أسرار الذات العالية، وستر أسرار الربوبية ليبقى الكنز مدفونا، والسر مصونا، ولولا هذا الطلسم لا فتضح السر، وناله من لا يستحقه، فيبتذل بالإظهار وينادَى عليه بلسان الاشتهار وهذا هو الرداء الذى أشار إليه فى الحديث «وما بين الناس وبين أن ينظروا إلى ربهم إلا رداء الكبرياء على وجهه فى جنة عدن» وهو رداء الحس والقهرية المنشور على وجه أسرار المعانى، وهذا فى حق أهل الحجاب فى الدنيا. وأما من زال عنه طلسم توحيد الذات فلا يحجب عنه الحق تعالى ساعة، لا فى الدنيا ولا فى الآخرة، فهم ينظرون إلى ذات الرحمن، فى كل أوان ويسمى هذا الطلسم عالم الفرق وعالم الحكمة وعالم الملك وعالم الأشباح وعالم الأثر ويسمى الكنز الذى ستر به عالم الجمع وعالم القدرة وعالم الملكوت وعالم الأرواح وعالم الغيب، وأما عالم الجبروت فهو البحر اللطيف الفياض الذى تتدفق

He added:

Listen to my words and absorb them,
If you understand:
Your treasure is now stripped
of any talisman.

Know thus that the presence of this talisman is real, that it is the will of Divine Wisdom that it protect the secrets both of the Supreme Essence and of Lordship, so that the Treasure might remain buried and the secret well guarded. If this talisman did not exist, the secret would be divulged and placed within reach of those who are not worthy of it; it would be exposed to the light of day, spread about in public. It is the curtain referred to in the *ḥadīth*: 'To keep men from casting their eyes upon their Lord, there is but the curtain of splendour lowered before His Face in the Garden of Eden.' This curtain is the curtain of the sensory world, of sovereign domination (*qahriyya*), drawn before the mysteries of intelligible realities. Such is the case, at least, in regard to the 'people of the veil' in this lower world. The God of Truth is not veiled, even for a moment, either in this world or in the other, from those for whom the talisman of the unity of Essence has been raised. They see the Essence of the All Merciful at all times.

This talisman has had a variety of names: the world of separation (*ʿālam al-farq*), the world of Wisdom, the world of the Kingdom (*mulk*), the world of bodies (*ashbāh*), the world of traces (*āthār*), the phenomenal world (*ʿālam al-shahāda*). And the Treasure it covers is called the world of union (*ʿālam al-jamʿ*), the world of Power (*qudra*), the world of Royalty (*malakūt*), the world of spirits (*arwāh*), the world of mystery (*ghayb*). As for the world of Omnipotence (*jabarūt*), it is the subtle, overflowing (*fayyāḍ*) Ocean from which all lights (the

منه أنوار الملكوت وهو عالم يقع به التجلي من الكنز المصون والسر المكنون. والحاصل أن الوجود واحد وهو وجود الحق تعالى، فما وقع به التجلي، من نظره بعين الجمع سماه ملكوتا، ومن نظره بعين الفرق في عالم الحكمة سماه مُلكا، وما لم يقع به التجلي من الأسرار اللطيفة الغيبية فهو جبروت، وهذا مجرد اصطلاح اللغة، فأهل الفرق من أهل الحجاب لا يرون إلا الملك، لوقوفهم مع حس الكائنات فاحتجبت عنهم أنوار الملكوت، وأهل الفناء لا يرون إلا الملكوت وتسرح أفكارهم في أسرار بحار الجبروت، وأهل البقاء يرون الملكوت ويسرحون في بحار الجبروت ويتنزلون إلى عالم الملك لأداء حقوق العبودية والأدب مع الربوبية ويتفننون في علومه فلا يحجبهم جمعهم عن فرقهم، ولا فرقهم عن جمعهم، ولا فناؤهم عن بقائهم، ولا بقاؤهم عن فنائهم، بل يعطون كل ذي حق حقه ويوفون كل ذي قسط قسطه. جعلنا الله من خواصهم بمنه وكرمه آمين وصلى الله على سيدنا محمد وعلى آله وصحبه وسلم تسليما والحمد لله رب العالمين.

manifestations of the Names and Attributes) of the world of Royalty shine forth; but, since it is not itself the place of manifestation (nor is it affected by manifestation), it belongs to the Hidden Treasure and to the well-guarded secret.

Thus, existence is unique; it is the very Existence of God (*al-ḥaqq*: the Real, the True, the Absolute). The place where manifestation takes place is referred to as 'Royalty' (*malakūt*) by whoever looks upon it with the eye of union (*ʿayn al-jamʿ*), while he who looks at it with the eye of separateness (*ʿayn al-farq*) in the world of Wisdom, calls it the 'Kingdom' (*mulk*). Where manifestation does not take place – the world of subtle secrets and mysteries – is referred to as 'Omnipotence' (*jabarūt*); but these names are nothing other than simple conventional denominations (*istilāh*). Those who look upon things as separate (those referred to as *ahl al-farq*), who are among the people of the veil, see nothing but the 'Kingdom', as they hold to the sensory aspect of beings and the lights of 'Royalty' are veiled from them. The people of extinction (*ahl al-fanāʿ*) see only 'Royalty', and their thoughts evolve freely into the unlimited secrets of 'Omnipotence'. The people of subsistence (or of perpetuation: *ahl al-baqāʿ*) see 'Royalty', evolve in the oceans of 'omnipotence', and descend (*yatanazzalūn*) back toward the world of the 'Kingdom' in order to finish the tasks inherent in the state of servitude, and to engage in proper behaviour toward the Lord, and to devote themselves diligently to the sciences related to these proper behaviours. For these individuals, the state of union is not a veil that hides the consciousness of separateness, and separateness is not a veil for union. Extinction is not a veil for subsistence, and subsistence is not a veil for extinction. They give each thing its due, and treat each thing in complete fairness. May God deign to include us among their elite, in His Grace and His Generosity. *Amīn*!

ملاحظات

١ في الأصل «المعتزلية».

٢ في الأصل «ناله» والصواب «ماله».

٣ في الأصل «قدر» والصواب «قد».

٤ أو «منكب» (محاسن ؟ – éd. Asin Palacios).

٥ أو «ذكرته» (ديوان الحلاج – éd. Massignon n° 52).

٦ أو «قتامه» (ديوان الحلاج – éd. Massignon n° 52).

NOTES

1 I have chosen to use this word to render the Arabic *tilsam,* or *talsam,* (pl. *talāsim*), throughout the text presented here. (The manuscripts often contain the forms *talsām, talāsīm,* which appear to be incorrect.) Ibn ʿAjība transposes the word, whose proper meaning has passed into French and English as 'talisman' (an object endowed with magical or supernatural virtues), in reference to the protective screens by which the Lord provisionally veils Himself from the eyes of creatures but which, like charms, can bring about a transformation of the human being such that his vision opens to the knowledge of essential reality that was originally hidden, and that he finds himself freed from certain illusory attributions or oppositions.

2 The word *lubb* (pl. *albāb*) refers to the seed, the flesh (of a fruit), and the heart, the spirit. In Sufi language, it is esoteric truth, in contrast to the letter of the law (*al-qishr,* the husk). The doubling here, for emphasis, might also be translated as 'the esoteric reality hidden in the depths of hearts'.

3 We see that Ibn ʿAjība is not reluctant to use this word: the past participle of the verb *halla,* which means 'reside, live, be situated', it has the same root as *hulūl,* 'incarnation' (of the Divinity in the human substrate), a word that was eschewed by the doctors of the law, just as was the doctrine for which it stood.

4 Cf. the *ḥadīth*: 'Seventy thousand of my nation will enter Paradise without being accountable. It is they who... will have surrendered entirely to God.' (Al-Bazzār; according to Anas, cited in Nabhānī, *Al-Fatḥ al-kabīr,* II, pp. 153–154).

5 ʿAbd al-Qādir al-Jaylānī (Gīlānī), the founder of the Qādiriyya, or Jalāla, Sufi order (b. 471/1079, d. in Baghdad 561/1166).

6 This *ḥadīth* appears in this form in Suyūṭī's *Jāmiʿ al-saghīr.*

7 'Habitually', because there are, of course, cases where man is deprived of his freedom to act because of fate (illness, for example) or through actions by his peers (imprisonment, or moral coercion).

8 Sahl al-Tustarī, a theologian and mystic, was al-Ḥallāj's first teacher; he was born in Tostar (Persia), where he died in 283/896.

9 *Ḥikam,* by Ibn ʿAṭāʾ Allāh al-Iskandarī.

10 Reported in Nabhānī, *Fatḥ al-kabīr,* I, pp. 422–423, according to *Jāmiʿ al-saghīr* (related by Abū Dāwūd).

11 *Kharq al-ʿāda,* literally 'breaking habits'. The expression refers to charismas, whether they are seen in the material order (*ḥissī*) or the immaterial order (*maʿnawī*); they are due to an exceptional and direct manifestation of *qudra* in the cosmic order (cf. above, p. 65, note 14).

12 Abū'l Husayn ʿAlī al-Shustarī, an Andalusian mystic born in Tina (7th/13th century), and is buried in Damiete. He was one of Ibn Sabʿīn's followers.

13 *Mashīshiyya.* The complete quote is 'And submerge me in the very Ocean of Unity, such that... etc.'

14 In his *Sahīh,* Bukhārī offers the following version of the *ḥadīth*, reported by Abū Hurayra: the Prophet said: God said, 'I shall declare war upon him who is hostile to one of my friends (*wali* = saint). My servant cannot approach me with anything that pleases Me more than what I have prescribed for him. And my servant does not stop drawing nearer to Me through voluntary devotions until I love him; and when I love him, I become the ear with which he hears, the eye with which he sees, the hand with which he strikes, and the foot with which he walks. If he asks me, I give to him, and if he seeks refuge in me, I protect him.'

15 Only the last three verses appear to have been penned by the Andalusian gnostic Ibn al-ʿIrrif (Ibn al-ʿArīf), who died in Marrakesh in 536/1141; the first two are from *Al-Hallāj* (according to L. Massignon, *Dīwān d'al-Ḥallāj,* 1931, pp. 86–87). Cf. also Ibn al-ʿArīf's *Mahāsin al-Majālis,* edited by Asín Palacios, Paris, 1933, p. 31 (translation) and p. 76 (Arabic text).